Safeguarding Electronic Information

This is the thirteenth in a McFarland series of Rutgers SCILS symposia under the general editorship of Jana Varlejs. The first twelve are *The Economics of Information* (1982), *The Right to Information* (1984), *Communication/Information/Libraries* (1985), *Freedom of Information and Youth* (1986), *Information Seeking* (1987), *Information and Aging* (1988), *Leadership in the Library/Information Profession* (1989), *Information Ethics* (1990), *Information Literacy* (1991), *Agents of Change* (1992), *Education for the Library/Information Profession* (1993) and *The Economics of Information in the 1990s* (1995).

*Proceedings of the Thirty-second Annual
Symposium of the Graduate Alumni and Faculty
of the Rutgers School of Communication,
Information and Library Studies, 21 April 1995*

Safeguarding Electronic Information

Edited by Jana Varlejs

McFarland & Company, Inc., Publishers
Jefferson, North Carolina, and London

Dedication: Elizabeth Futas (Rutgers Ph.D. 1980) died on February 6, 1995, during the midwinter conference of the American Library Association. She had directed the Graduate School of Library and Information Studies at the University of Rhode Island since 1986. She had also taught in the Emory and Rutgers library education programs, and had worked in the libraries of Queens College, Georgia State, and the Ford Foundation. Her scholarly and professional interests centered on collection development and women's status in librarianship, and she held various leadership positions in the American Library Association, including election to the executive board for 1984 to 1988. Outspoken, witty, and totally committed to the values of libraries and librarianship, Liz was a strong leader whose voice will be missed.

British Library Cataloguing-in-Publication data are available

Library of Congress Cataloguing-in-Publication data are available

Safeguarding electronic information : law and order on the Internet and other computer security quandries / edited by Jana Varlejs.
    p. cm.
    "Proceedings of the thirty-second annual symposium of the graduate alumni and faculty of the Rutgers School of Communication, Information and Library Studies, 21 April 1995."
    Includes bibliographical references and index.
    ISBN 0-7864-0189-3 (sewn softcover : 55# alk. paper) ∞
    1. Information networks—Law and legislation—United States—Congresses. 2. Data transmission systems—Law and legislation—United States—Congresses. 3. Data protection—Congresses.
4. Internet (Computer network)—Congresses. I. Varlejs, Jana.
II. Ruters University. School of Communication, Information and Library Studies.
KF2765.A2S24   1996
025.04—dc20   95-44767
                                             CIP

Manufactured in the United States of America

McFarland & Company, Inc., Publishers
 Box 611, Jefferson, North Carolina 28640

Table of Contents

Acknowledgments

Dr. Anne Ciliberti, president of the Graduate Alumni of the Rutgers School of Communication, Information and Library Studies, and Irene Percelli, vice president/president-elect, were closely involved in the planning of the symposium, and their contributions are much appreciated. For logistical help, we again owe thanks to Charlene Price Holder, coordinator of special events for the Rutgers Alumni Association. Special thanks go to speakers Marlyn Kemper Littman, Laura Lape, and Mike Godwin, and to moderator Jorge Reina Schement, who jointly made up for the absence of a fourth scheduled presenter. They provided us with an extended and lively discussion that was responsive to the audience's concerns and left listeners stimulated and informed.

1995 Honorary Alumni Award Citation

The annual symposium of the graduate alumni and faculty of the Rutgers School of Communication, Information and Library Studies usually is the occasion on which we recognize the achievements of one of our alumni through conferring the "Distinguished Alumni" award. In 1995, the alumni instead elected to confer honorary membership in the association upon Dr. Norman Horrocks. His retirement from the vice presidency of Scarecrow Press and from his visiting professorship in the Rutgers library and information studies program coincided with the end of the 1995 academic year, and therefore the presentation of the award also became a means of expressing our appreciation to him for his steadfast and invaluable service to Rutgers and our best wishes for the future. The citation presented on April 21st read as follows:

TRIBUTE TO DR. NORMAN HORROCKS

Whereas Dr. Norman Horrocks has served as visiting professor in the MLS program every semester and every summer since 1988, and thus has earned the right to the alias "staff," and

Whereas he has infused his classes with the wisdom and cosmopolitan outlook gained in a career spanning nearly half a century and three continents, and

Whereas not only his students and colleagues at Rutgers, but also many New Jersey librarians have benefited from his experience as librarian, educator, parliamentarian, writer, and publisher, as well as from his leadership in a wide variety of professional associations, and

Whereas the Rutgers SCILS community will feel the loss of Dr. Horrocks' counsel and good humor, and surely will miss being the first to hear the latest,

Therefore, be it resolved, that the Graduate Alumni of the Rutgers School of Communication, Information and Library Studies bestow upon Norman Horrocks honorary membership in the Association, with all the rights and privileges accorded thereto, and

Be it further resolved, that this distinction be spread upon the minutes of this Association and be made known to the profession.

Introduction:
Danger and Opportunity
on the Electronic Frontier

Jana Varlejs

This introductory essay serves as both a preface to and an extension of the proceedings of the 1995 Rutgers School of Communication, Information and Library Studies (SCILS) symposium. First, I explain the selection and scope of the symposium topic. Next, I review the dominant concerns that were voiced by the speakers and audience. Along the way, I refer to resources that give readers avenues toward further exploration of specific issues. Finally, I place these concerns within a larger framework of information policy problems.

Background

In 1994, it seemed as if a new kind of crime wave had crested. The crimes themselves were of the traditional mayhem-and-larceny variety, but their *modus operandi* required state-of-the-art computer equipment and expertise. Hardly a week passed without reports of theft and fraud executed electronically, or defamation and pornography dispensed via the Internet. The euphoria of computer users discovering the rewards of connectivity and the vast riches of the "information superhighway" gave way to anxiety about viruses infecting their machines, pedophiles seducing their children over the Internet, E-mail eavesdroppers, and misappropriated personal information and intellectual property. The realization that the electronic global village was no safer than the real world was followed by the inevitable reaction, that is, the urge to regulate. One example is

Senator Exon's "communication decency" amendment to the telecommunication bill of 1995; another is the effort to create patent protection for computer software.[1] Meanwhile, a Clinton administration task force has been working on the second version of its report on intellectual property and the National Information Infrastructure (NII).[2]

If a common theme can be said to have emerged from these varied concerns, it is security. Institutional electronic files are increasingly accessible on a dial-in basis, and are therefore vulnerable to unauthorized perusal and manipulation. Personal and mass communication over electronic networks can be appropriated in ways not intended by the initiators. "Electronic frontier," a popular name for the Internet, is apt, implying not only the adventure of exploring new territory but also the danger of a zone of no established law and order. Since personal data about almost everyone in this country resides in one sort of electronic database or another, the question of who can get at that data and what can be done with such data is of very wide interest. Hence, the topic of computer security, broadly construed, seemed an appropriate choice for the first symposium directed not only toward our traditional library/information community, but also toward the wider community of all Rutgers School of Communication, Information and Library Studies students and alumni.[3]

"Safeguarding Electronic Information" was chosen as the umbrella title for the 1995 symposium in an effort to encompass not only technical aspects of security, but also the ethical issues of personal privacy, intellectual property protection, and censorship. As moderator Jorge Reina Schement pointed out, what was really under discussion was information policy. He saw one of the papers presented as covering an aspect of privacy, another property, and a third communication—"the three legs of the information policy stool."

As originally planned, the symposium's first speaker was to have been Thomas Blanton of the National Security Archive, a non-governmental, non-profit institute that promotes open government. As editor of *White House E-Mail: The Top Secret Messages the Reagan/Bush White House Thought They Had Destroyed* (New York: The New Press, 1995), Blanton was to have addressed the issues related to the Archive's work to secure electronic governmental communication for posterity just as paper and audio records have been. The idea was to highlight the tensions between network users' desire for privacy versus the public interest in freedom of information, as well as the technical aspects of the security of electronic versus paper based communication. Sadly, a last-minute emergency prevented Blanton's participation. The reader is referred to his book, and to the press, which regularly chronicles the growth of electronic communication and the attendant issues of security, privacy, and censorship.

Computer Security

It was the computer security problems that Marlyn Kemper Littman was asked to expound. This was a charge she carried out by documenting cases of invasion of computer systems, from academic to commercial. After describing typical kinds of incursions, she outlined protective measures, emphasizing the need for constant vigilance and use of multiple strategies. Handing out rolls of Certs mints to the audience, Littman ensured that we would remember to call C.E.R.T. (the Computer Emergency Response Team) to report security breaches and to obtain information and help!

The rise in computer crime is a logical result of the growth of computer ownership and participation in electronic networks. Some see this situation as out of control, with the technology beating the legal system's ability to keep pace. According to lawyers Friedman, Carmicino, and Buys, making good computer crime laws is seen as difficult, but both the federal and almost all state governments have enacted such statutes.[4] These lawyers also stress the fact that the Internet respects no national borders, which complicates everything. Nevertheless, they call for new efforts to develop appropriate legislation:

> Finally, the law has traditionally concerned itself with the regulation of tangible things and tangible beings. In the future, the best way to prevent "cybercrimes" will be "cyberlaws"; that is, laws written specifically to combat crimes on the Internet.[5]

As an educator, Marlyn Kemper Littman was not thinking about computer crime in terms of law and prosecution, but rather in terms of prevention based on understanding and current awareness. In addition to subscribing to the C.E.R.T. listserv, as she suggests, it would seem prudent for library automation staff to scan not only the pertinent library/ information science literature, but also computer science literature, such as *The Computer Security Handbook*[6] and publications of the Association for Computing Machinery (acmhelp@acm.org). The wide range of information available at all levels of sophistication is exemplified by the *LC Science Tracer Bullet* on computer security.[7]

Intellectual Property
in the Electronic Environment

The property leg of the information-policy stool was addressed by Syracuse College of Law professor Laura Lape, who used the NII task force's draft report on intellectual property as a jumping-off point for an explication of copyright law and its application in the electronic environment. Lape emphasized the importance of the principle underlying copyright law; i.e., the goal is to make ideas, information, creative works, and so on, available to the public. The specific protections governing reproduction and other uses do not imply a constitutional, "inalienable" right, and are not in the same category as rights to physical property. The ideal balance between adequate profit incentive to create works and public access to those works should not be jettisoned just because a work is in digital form or is transmitted via an electronic network. Lape's views suggest that librarians are too readily swayed in the direction of the producer's urge to protect rather than the public's interest in access. Her statement that fair use is determined on a case-by-case basis and therefore should not be relied on so heavily should spark a re-examination of the profession's interpretation of copyright law.[8]

The First Amendment in Cyberspace

The third leg of Schement's information-policy stool—communication—was the subject of Mike Godwin's presentation. As counsel for the Electronic Frontier Foundation, Godwin is an unabashed advocate of free speech rights, and he interprets the First Amendment broadly. Using analogy and contrast, he clarified what is new and different about the electronic environment and what is not, and put the governmental urge to regulate in historical context.

During the discussion period, the question of children's access to pornography on the Internet was raised. Littman reported that she had observed very careful monitoring of children's use of the Net in some schools, but that other schools were teaching children to be good cybercitizens and urging parents to play a similar positive role. Appendix D contains a statement of principles that can form the basis for such educational efforts. Frank W. Connolly, from whom the statement is available, believes that school boards, school administrators, and teachers need to model ethical behavior and to implement appropriate policies so that young people will learn to become responsible computer users.[9] For an example, see the *School Library Journal* article which includes one school's very specific "Technology Code of Conduct."[10]

In addition to reliance on education and parental persuasion, children's computer access to undesirable material might be controlled through technical means. While no one had specific information to contribute at the time, in the months since the symposium took place, at least one product has become commercially available. This is Surfwatch, which has been the subject of considerable discussion on the American Library Association's Office of Intellectual Freedom's listserv. The software is designed to "lock" online sites that contain sexually explicit material, and thus gives adults a way to limit what children can access. Since censorship is repugnant to advocates of intellectual freedom, quite a number of negative comments have appeared on the listserv. Especially troubling to some is that it is not entirely clear what criteria are used to select sites to be censored. Meanwhile, other products are in the development stage.[11]

It is not only sexually oriented communication that worries parents and educators, however. For example, it is possible to download items such as *The School Stopper's Textbook*, "which tells how to short-circuit electrical wiring, set off explosives in school plumbing and 'break into your school at night and burn it down,'" according to Stephen Bates.[12] Other examples he cites are files on suicide methods, drug archives, and information on how to break and enter computer networks, cash machines, etc. Bates describes measures used by schools to guard against censorship imposed from outside, such as parental consent forms.

More Legal Questions

Another issue that received considerable attention during the symposium's discussion period was intellectual property rights. To what extent do you worry about excerpts from other works that you want to incorporate in your home page? What about the links? What protection do you have against others scanning your publication, perhaps altering it in some way, and posting it on the Internet? Are you breaking the law when you download information that is copyrighted, but has been posted on the Internet for anyone to use? On this latter point, Lape faults the "Fair Use in the Electronic Age" document (Appendix A) developed by representatives of a number of library associations. She says that the document implies that this action would fall under the rubric of "fair use"—a bad idea, because individuals have not been held liable for using infringing material, and also because of the way fair use is treated in the courts.

Other concerns about potential personal and institutional liability resulting from electronic network use were expressed. In a number of cases, the answers are ambiguous. While current law seems to apply perfectly well most of the time, there are problematic areas. Thus, while Lape appears to find existing intellectual property law adequate (or at least better than the changes proposed by the NII Working Group), Godwin is not so sure.

The library/information specialist who wishes to disentangle the copyright issues will want to begin with the new edition of *The Copyright Primer for Librarians and Educators* (see note 8), while keeping Lape's focus on the public interest balance in mind. In addition to the items listed in the bibliography of the *Primer*, it is advisable to consider the international perspective, as the Internet recognizes no borders.[13] See, for example, an article by Sandy Norman, the copyright advisor for the International Federation of Library Associations and Institutions.[14] She uses the term "electrocopying" as defined by the International Federation of Reproduction Rights Owners: "the storage, display, dissemination, manipulation or reproduction of printbase copyright works into machine-readable form," which means:

- Using an optical scanner or document image processor to digitize copyright protected works;
- Rekeying such works from paper format into a word-processor;
- Downloading from an online database, floppy disk or CD-Rom into a paper format;
- Downloading from databases directly onto a computer;
- Sending copyright electronic material around a local area network;
- Sending such works by e-mail or even fax.[15]

She says that all of these are restricted acts, and that despite the laissez faire of the Internet, "librarians must be seen to respect copyright," even though they do not pose the major threat to copyright owners that the public at large does. Nelson feels that new controls are necessary in order to make electronic publishing viable (because electronic publishing *is* in the public interest), and thus she is on the side of those who think that additional or different legislation is necessary. Laura Lape would say that Norman's view is overly protective of the industry at the expense of the user. See also Laura Gasaway's comments on scanning in *Library Journal*.[16]

Information Policy

The stakes in this balancing act are very high, as the merging of communication technologies of all sorts is bound to continue, with or without the kind of policy advice that the Clinton administration's Information Infrastructure Task Force is intended to provide. As Weingarten points out in the paper reprinted in Appendix B, the views of the organizations that are the likely builders of the physical infrastructure are shaped by a very different history and culture from those of the users. He makes a strong case for an appropriate government role in ensuring "that two diverse public interests are protected: (1) The need for broad public access to the dominant knowledge and communication streams in our society, [and] (2) The right of individuals to enjoy privacy in their communications and to freely contract among themselves for the sale or exchange of information goods and services."[17]

Weingarten's paper is useful in placing discussions such as those held at the Rutgers symposium within the larger context of the current debates over telecommunication and information policy. Similarly useful is Carroll's book on personal records in electronic databases, which includes a lengthy list of legislation pertinent to privacy/security issues and demonstrates that "privacy," like "information," is a multifaceted and complex concept.[18]

In his introduction to the Rutgers symposium, moderator Schement reminded the audience that in the United States, a consensus on national information policy has never been achieved. After considering the complexities discussed during this symposium and reading the policy development document in Appendix B, one might be tempted to conclude that a consensus is even more elusive today than it was some decades ago.[19] On the other hand, the widely visible challenges posed by the electronic frontier are getting the attention of policy makers as never before. The Clinton administration's idea of a "National Information Infrastructure" seems to build on earlier plans for the National Research and Education Network (NREN), and Speaker of the House Gingrich has declared himself a supporter of the "information superhighway." But even as the NII idea was being developed into concrete proposals by a special task force, Congress proceeded with telecommunications legislation likely to make at least some of the NII discussion moot.

Perhaps the ideal of a carefully formulated and consensual national information policy is unrealistic. The very concept of an information policy is elusive, depending on who is talking to whom, and how "information" is defined. Sharon Martin argues that the failure to differentiate between "information" as carrier and as content in legislation such as the Freedom of Information Act and the Computer Security Act has created a muddle that ultimately endangers access.[20]

Information policy as an area of study is a relatively recent phenomenon, and its scope is not defined consistently. As Burger suggests, the best approach may be to look at

> effects of information control ... not the efficient management of information resources.... How available information is controlled, who controls it, and why it is controlled in the way it is are questions whose answers will determine the health of the body politic in the years to come.[21]

Defining information policy in terms of control helps one to focus on the parameters of this amorphous area and to construct a framework for examining its various facets. While the Rutgers symposium dealt with only some of the issues germane to information policy, it illustrated vividly the importance of seeing these issues within their larger social and political context. If information professionals are to bring their expertise to bear on the current discussions involving infrastructure and problems of access in a new electronic environment, they need to understand the perspective of others who have different stakes in the control of information.

Figure 1 represents an attempt to visualize the information policy arena and to identify major players. The array of interested parties from the for-profit sector looks especially formidable in light of the $864 billion figure attached to them in a report cited in Appendix B. The information industry's counterparts in the public sector and the various groups and alliances spawned in part or in whole by the Internet are finding it difficult to have an impact on decisions affecting information access. Ironically, the inclination of Congress to deregulate the communication technology industry is matched by the urge to regulate the contents of communication transmitted by the technology. Deregulation is intended to increase competition, which in turn should lead to decreased prices for consumers in the long run, and the First Amendment remains a bulwark against freedom of speech assaults. Nevertheless, the policies being developed may lead to disenfranchisement of the many people who lack the affluence and the technical skills to take advantage of the "information superhighway," and may result in monitoring and censorship of Internet use.

To gain insights into why information policy formulation is so problematic, read Jorge Schement's recent book, *Tendencies and Tensions of the Information Age* (see note 22). Schement and coauthor Terry Curtis

```
┌─────────────────────────────────────────────────────────────────┐
│                    INFORMATION POLICY                             │
│                 How is information controlled?                    │
│                      Who controls it?                             │
│              Why is it controlled in the way it is?*              │
│                                                                   │
│        INFORMATION              POLICY                            │
│                                                                   │
│        Types:                   Issues:                           │
│          Scientific/Scholarly     Privacy                         │
│          Government               Intellectual property           │
│          Commercial               Equitable access               │
│          Artistic                 Free speech                     │
│          Personal                 National security              │
│                                                                   │
│        Roles:                   Stakeholders:                     │
│          Social                   Government                      │
│          Economic                 Business/Industry               │
│          Cultural                 Education/Research              │
│                                   General public                  │
│                                                                   │
│        Dimensions:              Mechanisms:                       │
│          Local                    Legislation                     │
│          National                 Regulatory agencies             │
│          Global                   Judicial system                 │
│                                   Marketplace                     │
│                                   Press                           │
│                                   Libraries/Archives              │
│                                   Public interest watchdogs       │
│                                                                   │
│ *See note 21.                                                     │
└─────────────────────────────────────────────────────────────────┘
```

Figure 1. A framework for thinking about information policy.

suggest that much misunderstanding is due to failure to learn from history and blindness to underlying assumptions Americans have about their economy and government. The practice of letting each new technology generate new policy ignores the lessons to be learned from the development of, for example, the postal service and the telephone.[22] The assumptions that complicate any discussion of policy that involves balancing private interests and the public good are: the public's consumer needs should be paramount, government should not interfere with the marketplace, competition should be maximal, the courts are the place to resolve differences between public and private interests, and government is less efficient than the private sector.[23] Because there are contradictions inherent in these assumptions, it is not surprising that consensus eludes policy makers. As Schement and Curtis put it, "were Americans to pay more attention to their own underlying beliefs, they would see a lack of a coherent national information policy as neither arbitrary nor directionless."[24] One would like to think that the present debates about whether new legislation and regulation is needed to control the dangers of the electronic frontier could be turned into an opportunity to think more clearly and holistically about information policy in general.

References

1. Sabra Chartrand, "U.S. proposes guidelines in an attempt to deal more effectively with software inventions," *The New York Times*, 5 June 1995, D2.

2. U.S. Department of Commerce, *Intellectual Property and the National Information Infrastructure: A Preliminary Draft of the Report of the Working Group on Intellectual Property Rights*, July 1994 (also known as "the green paper"; final report expected in August 1995).

3. The School offers undergraduate majors in journalism/mass media and in communication; masters programs in library service and in communication and information studies; and, with the Graduate School, a cross-disciplinary doctoral program. In May 1995, the School conducted for the first time its own separate graduation ceremony for all its graduates, and the Graduate Alumni of SCILS is being reorganized to include all the School's graduates. The annual symposium in 1995, therefore, deals with issues of interest to the entire SCILS constituency. These proceedings, however, reflect the transition, giving greater attention to concerns of the library community.

4. Marc S. Friedman, Benedict G. Carmencino, and Kenneth R. Buys, "Infojacking: Crimes on the Information Superhighway," *New Jersey Law Journal* 140 (May 22, 1995): S-2.

5. *Ibid.*, S-3.

6. Richard H. Baker, *Computer Security Handbook*, 2d ed. (Blue Ridge Summit, PA: TAB, 1991).

7. Michelle Cadoree, "Computer Crime and Security," *LC Science Tracer Bulletin* TB 94-1 (March 1994). Available from Science and Technology Division, Library of Congress, 10 First St., S.E., Washington, D.C. 20540-5580.

8. See, for example, Janis H. Bruwelheide, *The Copyright Primer for Librarians and Educators*, 2d ed. (Chicago: American Library Association, 1995), 11–15, on the fair use doctrine in the library context. See also note 16 and Appendix A.

9. Frank W. Connolly, "Intellectual Honesty in the Era of Computing," *T.H.E. Journal* 22 (April 1995): 86–88.

10. Bruce Flanders, "A Delicate Balance," *School Library Journal* 40 (October 1994): 34.

11. Steve Lohr, "The Net: It's Hard to Clean Up," *The New York Times*, 18 June 1995, sec. 4.

12. Stephen Bates, "The Next Frontier in the Book Wars," *The New York Times*, 6 November 1994, Education Life supplement, 22–23.

13. For a European perspective, see Anita L. Morse, review of *Information Transfer Policy: Issues of Control and Access*, by Tamara S. Eisenschitz, *Library and Information Science Research* 17 (Winter 1995): 92–95.

14. Sandy Norman, "Electronic Copyright: The Issues." *IFLA Journal* 20, no. 2 (1994): 171–75.

15. *Ibid.*, 171–72.

16. Laura N. Gasaway, "The Great Copyright Debate," *Library Journal* 119 (September 15, 1994): 34–37.

17. See Appendix B.

18. John M. Carroll, *Confidential Information Sources: Public and Private*, 2d ed. (Boston: Butterworth-Heinemann, 1991).

19. Jana Varlejs, ed., *The Right to Information* (Jefferson, NC: McFarland, 1984), v–vii.

20. Sharon E. Martin, *Bits, Bytes, and Big Brother: Federal Information Control in the Technological Age* (Westport, CT: Praeger, 1995).

21. Robert H. Burger, *Information Policy: A Framework for Evaluation and Policy Research* (Norwood, NJ: Ablex, 1993), 174.

22. Jorge Reina Schement and Terry Curtis, *Tendencies and Tensions of the Information Age: The Production and Distribution of Information in the United States* (New Brunswick, NJ: Transaction, 1995), 142.

23. *Ibid.*, 164–65.

24. *Ibid.*, 166.

Protecting Electronic Data:
A Losing Battle?

Marlyn Kemper Littman

Computer networks support innovative applications that include tele-commuting, videoconferencing, distance education, virtual offices, virtual universities and collaborative learning environments. As a result of these capacities, computer networks can transform ways in which we communicate, interact and discover new knowledge domains. The communications technologies enabling users to reach beyond their desktops to take advantage of the Internet and other online services make these networks susceptible to invasion by crackers also known as cyberhackers, cyber-thieves, cyberpunks and network terrorists.

During the Gulf War, cyberhackers from Holland infiltrated U.S. Department of Defense computers. Thirty-four sites were affected. In some cases, data linked to military operations were altered. Reportedly, GE, Motorola and the North American Air Defense Command have experienced network break-ins. Crackers blocking weather forecasts to a ship in the English Channel through a network invasion were blamed by Scotland Yard for loss of life at sea.

Last year, a hacker accessed the GEAC system at the University of Southern Mississippi library via the Internet; escaped through a loophole into UNIX, the operating environment in which GEAC is mounted; modified software and group permissions; and set up his own directory on the library network.[1] By pretending to be an authorized user, the hacker had the capability to do a great deal of serious damage both to the library network and to remote locations. These incidents illustrate the vulnerability of any individual computer network connected to the information superhighway.

While my comments focus in substantial part on the library environment, the same challenges are applicable wherever computers are linked to a network. As Dr. B. R. Black, Director of Information Technology of the Polk County (Florida) School System, warns: "The problem with Internet access is, anytime I can get out, I know a cracker can get in."[2]

Greg Rivera, Jr., Systems Librarian for the Tampa Bay Library Consortium, noted: "A good hacker could probably break-in to our system and from there infiltrate other areas of the Internet. Internet gateways used by organizations to connect internal networks to others serve as open doors to intruders as well."[3]

Stories on the hazards of network security appear regularly in the *New York Times*, *Washington Post*, *Wall Street Journal*, *Time* and *Newsweek* and on such top rated television shows as *60 Minutes*. Yet, when I recently raised the issue of network security with colleagues in libraries, I received the following responses:

- "We are too small. Nobody would be interested in our network."
- "We know we need to do something, but who has the time?"
- "Our files are read-only. We are immune to attacks."
- "You are making me nervous."

From these remarks, it appears that recognition of the importance of network security in the library setting is to say the least erratic.[4] Security efforts are often constrained by lack of information, funding, personnel and time.

How can we be sure that our networks are reasonably resistant to attacks? Are we protected against killer break-ins? My presentation addresses security challenges and includes reports of my case study research with colleagues throughout the country on the multidimensional aspects of network security. During this presentation, we will examine:

- Security problems.
- Approaches for safeguarding information resources.
- Guidelines for the development and implementation of a security policy.

Security Problems

Security problems occur with more frequency than we are willing to acknowledge. Alan Liddle, lieutenant commander in the Royal Navy and professor of systems management at the National Defense University (NDU), told me that intruders "visited" NDU very soon after the institution went on the Internet.[5] Lieutenant Commander Liddle said: "Collecting the evidence on how big and frequent break-ins are is extraordinarily difficult;

but even a conservative extrapolation from those reported indicates the problem is significant."

In January 1994, the College Center for Library Automation in Tallahassee identified a disruption in the LINCC online system connecting Florida's twenty-eight community colleges. The problem was traced to a public access terminal in the library at St. Petersburg Junior College. Dr. Susan Anderson, library director at St. Petersburg Junior College, related that through the use of this terminal, students broke into a little-known portion of the LINCC program.[6] Subsequently, they issued a system command to identify and save all titles starting with the word "the" in a file they created on the college's mainframe. This action reduced system response time and potentially could block operations throughout the entire network. According to Anderson, the students were apprehended by local police, and she commented, "I can only imagine what could happen when we are connected to the Internet."

Crackers penetrate computer networks with lightning speed. Often we cannot detect who commits security violations. Computer crimes such as embezzlement, burglary, software piracy and fraud can be committed by organized gangs, computer masterminds, angry workers, or furious ex-employees. Incursions may be identified but not reported. It's embarrassing to admit publicly to a network invasion.

Internet Invasions

The Internet began as a U.S. government research project and now links tens of millions of users in an estimated 150 countries. The goal of the Internet is worldwide connectivity. As we have seen, a consequence of global internetworking is that every network linked to the Internet is vulnerable to invasion. Internet invasions take place in various ways.

Air Force Major William F. Conroy III, a system software engineer with the United States Transportation Command, said: "The most significant threats to systems connected to the Internet are not related to damage to particular files; rather the greatest threats relate to loss of system control."[7] Major Conroy told me that read-protecting files on a library system can prevent an invader from changing data resident in these files. However, read-only files provide no protection against actions of a cyberhacker who invades the operating system via Internet access. By masquerading as a legitimate superuser, a hacker can gain the power not only to read files but also to overwrite or destroy virtually any file.

Brett Kemper is head of automated systems for Florida's Broward County Library. He said that the library's online public access catalog contains read-only files.[8] However, the Novell NetWare operating environment in which the OPAC functions is vulnerable to security breaches. Crackers involved in a Novell NetWare break-in could crash the library network.

There are any number of ways to invade a system. Spoofing is one of them. Spoofing involves fooling a target computer into believing that a message is coming from a friendly source. This technique was used by alleged Internet infiltrator Kevin Mitnick to steal files and software in a Christmas Day attack in 1994 on the workstation of a computer security researcher at the San Diego Supercomputer Center. Prior to his recent arrest, Mitnick had the dubious distinction of being on the FBI's Most Wanted list.

During the spoofing attack, legitimate users may encounter strange network operations such as a blank window that will no longer respond to their commands or commands that they did not enter appearing on their terminals. Once the attack is completed, spoofing is extremely hard to detect. After gaining root access in a spoofing penetration, the invader can masquerade as a legitimate user and access remote hosts.

Spoofing is not regarded as a threat to governmental agencies with networks containing classified information operating outside the Internet. These agencies can restrict Internet connectivity.

This approach is not workable in a university operating in a distributed computing environment. In an educational setting, an Internet link provides access to valuable information and an instant communications pathway. The risks, however, can be high. Dr. John Scigliano is vice president for academic computing and information technology at Nova Southeastern University. He told me that cyberhackers using Internet utilities such as FTP, e-mail, Telnet, finger, the World Wide Web, and Gopher have tried to invade the Nova network.[9] Identification and authentication services aid in blocking these assaults. A combination of network management products and software tools is used routinely to monitor the Nova system.

Another technique for launching an invasion is exploiting the capabilities of free network management products on the Internet. The Security Administrator Tool for Analyzing Networks, SATAN, is now available at no cost on the Internet. With SATAN, network administrators can probe for and report security loopholes at networked computer sites. Co-developer of SATAN Dan Farmer argues the tool's ready availability is intended as an aid for protection. However, he admits that SATAN could be used by an infocriminal seeking to exploit a security weakness. Reportedly, Farmer's employers at Silicon Graphics disagreed with Farmer's decision to distribute the program as shareware via the Internet. The company noted that hackers with time on their hands could use SATAN as a weapon for network incursions. Farmer and Silicon Graphics parted ways.

Greg Horne is manager of Academic Computing and Strategic Technologies at Nova. He said: "In preparing for possible SATAN incursions, we have battened down the hatches and are getting ready for the storm."[10]

According to Lieutenant Commander Liddle, damages from network break-ins can range from approximately $65,000 to $250,000 a year depending on what you have on your network. He noted that if your network is used by a hacker to penetrate other networks you could be responsible for damages incurred and this dollar amount could be exorbitant.[11]

Viruses

Another threat to network security is the computer virus. A virus is a malicious code that is buried within a program. After the program is executed, the virus code is activated and replicates itself by infecting other programs in a computer or throughout a network. Viruses require a host and can originate in new or repackaged software, freeware, shareware, leased computers, or computers recently returned from a repair shop.

Internet bulletin boards are also a source for disseminating various viral strains. Reportedly, thousands of users of *alt.binaries.pictures.erotica*, a popular Internet BBS (bulletin board system), unknowingly downloaded sexually explicit shareware, infected with the kaos4 virus, posted by a cracker. The result was lost data and file corruption.

Dr. Jeanine Gendron is technology specialist at Coconut Creek High School in Coconut Creek, Florida. She pointed out that an effective method for preventing potential viral attacks is loading an anti-virus software package on a computer as soon as it is deployed in an institutional setting.[12]

Donald Hyatt is director of the computer systems lab at Thomas Jefferson High School for Science and Technology in Alexandria, Virginia. He commented that as part of the virus prevention plan at his high school, students are not allowed to bring floppy disks from home containing computer games to the school computer lab since these games frequently contain viruses.[13] The publicity accompanying such viruses as Michelangelo, Stoned, and Green Caterpillar underscores the importance of adhering to virus prevention policies.

The Jerusalem virus was introduced into the CD-ROM LAN at the Broward County Main Library in Fort Lauderdale, Florida. Brett Kemper said: "We locked the floppy drives. This action created an uproar among patrons who preferred to download data onto diskettes instead of sitting at terminals and printing everything out."[14] This experience illustrates the challenge of balancing restrictions through physical security barriers on the one hand and optimal user access on the other.

Worms

A worm is another threat to computer security. A worm is an automated program that through replication uses up networking resources until eventually the network shuts down. A security loophole leaving the World Wide Web and its graphical interface Mosaic vulnerable to a worm was uncovered in February 1995. Hackers taking advantage of this flaw could bring Web services on the Internet to a halt. The National Center for Supercomputing Applications at the University of Illinois which developed Mosaic has created a software patch to correct this flaw.

Privacy Assaults

Privacy is yet another security concern. The Internet is a global information network supporting the worldwide exchange and distribution of sensitive information. This information can include home addresses, birthdays, telephone numbers, social security numbers, medical records, financial statements and financial transactions. Without effective safeguards, this information can be made available improperly to governmental, commercial and even criminal interception in violation of an individual's right to privacy.

Privacy protection also involves preserving information integrity so that hackers are prevented from maliciously tampering with personal data online. In response to my question on the frequency and seriousness of this type of violation on the Internet, Lieutenant Commander Liddle noted that an individual intent on causing damage could begin in the morning and "have a DUI [Driving Under the Influence] charge on your driver's license" by the afternoon.[15]

At this moment, scores of Internet shoppers buying merchandise at Internet cybermalls are sending their credit card numbers via the information superhighway to online vendors. Since the Internet is an open medium, the transfer of unprotected credit card information is risky and subject to release through wiretapping and line monitoring to unauthorized intruders. Recently, alleged Internet infiltrator Kevin Mitnick stole twenty thousand credit card numbers off of a commercial computer network. Security solutions currently under consideration to deter credit card theft include the use of encryption techniques, personal identification numbers and personal payment passwords.

Approaches for Safeguarding Information Resources

A secure network system supports information confidentiality and reliable message delivery throughout all network nodes. Security involves minimizing exposure of assets and resources to modification, corruption and unauthorized disclosure. In their book *Firewalls and Internet Security*, William Cheswick and Steven Bellovin point out that security involves preventing individuals "from doing things you do not want them to do to, with, on, or from" your computer or your peripheral devices.[16]

Generally, network security is a tradeoff with expedience. Most users seem willing to accept a higher level of risk rather than forgo network access to worldwide information resources. Yet, security policies that protect information resources from assaults are indispensable. In pointing out that prevention is the best security approach, Scigliano noted: "You have to determine what level of damage is acceptable and then build your security system from there."[17]

Authentication

A security system allows authorized users to access network resources. Provision of network access control, particularly in a distributed computing environment, is challenging. Since any security scheme can be broken, the notion of security products protecting a computer network from all forms of unauthorized access is illusory.

Dr. William Piotrowski, chief of information services with the Leon County (Florida) School Board, told me: "The prudent thing is try to be proactive. Because of the nature of the technology we are dealing with, I don't think anybody's network is truly secure."[18]

Electronic messages can be monitored and picked up at unsecured gateways. Traffic analyzers can be used to capture login and password sequences. Break-ins can also be initiated over dial-up phone lines so that intruders can capture confidential information on legitimate users.

Since a determined hacker can successfully infiltrate even a well protected network, procedures for distinguishing between users and computer services that may be trusted and those that may not are essential.

Authentication mechanisms such as passwords, encryption and digital signatures allow users and resources to be identified as trusted entities.

Passwords

The most common security mechanism is the use of passwords, yet many users do not take their passwords seriously. Passwords are often considered an inconvenience.

A password is a code that identifies an authorized user and indicates which network operations can be performed. A password should not be placed in an online file, easily guessed, written down and hidden in a top desk drawer, or pasted on a computer monitor. Unencrypted passwords sent through unsecured e-mail across communications lines can readily be captured by network monitoring tools or sniffers.

When selecting passwords, computer users are remarkably uncreative. Typically, users select passwords that are meaningful in terms of their lifestyles. They choose family names, pet names and birthdays. Careless password selection and use are leading causes of network incursions.

To identify passwords, cybercrackers can run commercially available password cracking programs such as NETCRACK or PASSTEST or try every entry in a dictionary. Crackers can also penetrate systems by using borrowed or shared passwords, capturing passwords through a network analyzer as users log onto the system or tapping into accounts for a "visitor" or "guest" which do not have passwords assigned.

Password interception is becoming commonplace on the Internet. As a result of break-ins at Rice University and the University of California, thousands of passwords were stolen. A team of intruders invaded the Texas A&M University network with the aid of a password cracking program and then set up an illegal bulletin board for information exchange.

Tactics for ensuring network integrity against password attacks in an Internet environment include deactivating old accounts, password encryption, restricting users to one log-on at a time, prohibiting the re-use of previously selected passwords, limiting the number of inaccurate log-on attempts and establishing a mechanism for reporting password violations. At Rutgers, users are required to change their passwords periodically or else they are dropped from the network. At Nova, users are limited to three incorrect log-ons.

Another technique minimizing network damage is the use of dial-back modems in conjunction with password protection. After a valid password has been entered, the answering modem dials back the authorized user to establish an online session.

Firewalls

Beyond passwords, there is a growing security technology including firewalls, encryption and biometric devices.

James Litchko is director of business development for Trusted Information Systems. He said: "Although the benefits of Internet connection can be enormous, the risks can be as great. An effective and practical means of network protection is an Internet firewall."[19]

Firewall is the term applied to a powerful network security tool consisting of hardware and software that allow your organization access to Internet resources while prohibiting unwanted incursions from the Internet into your organization. Firewalls support incoming services such as FTP, log-ins and e-mail while providing protection against intruders.

With a firewall, you can monitor outbound communications and create a detailed audit trail of all attempted and successful log-ons. Firewalls offer strong protection between your organization and the outside world and also can be used internally to keep users away from confidential information and selected databases and applications. Firewalls can be pricey. The cost of a firewall in use at Wells Fargo is $40,000. However, firewalls are commercially available for as little as $15,000.

Even firewalls are not invulnerable. The now infamous adventures of Kevin Mitnick involved invasion of a system that was protected by a firewall.

Encryption

Encryption or coding keeps information transmitted via a communications link safe from unauthorized access and tampering.

The encryption process involves converting the original message (plaintext) into an unreadable form (ciphertext) through the use of an encoding algorithm by the authorized sender. When the resulting ciphertext is sent across the network, would-be eavesdroppers using taps and network analyzers can collect the ciphertext but cannot unscramble the material. Decryption occurs when the intended recipient reconverts the ciphertext back into the original plaintext with the use of a key. A key is a string of digital information allowing users to encode or decode a message.

In traditional cryptography, two parties share the same secret key to code and decode messages. The strength of an encryption system depends on the ability of designated users to protect the key from outside access. Since shared keys are transmitted or communicated either online or through surface mail, the possibility exists that these keys can be intercepted by would-be crackers. If keys are inadvertently misplaced, the encrypted information is unsalvageable as well. Keys are difficult to memorize. They are often shared with others, thereby placing the information in jeopardy.

There are a number of more or less sophisticated encryption and decryption systems. The success of any of these systems is limited by the degree to which the distribution of the encoding and decoding keys is protected.

Leading algorithms for encoding information are DES (Data Encryption Standard) and RSA. The latter name stands for the initials of the individuals who invented the code, namely Ronald Rivest, Adi Shamir and Leonard Addleman. Commercial software products using RSA are available from Lotus, IBM, Sun, Digital, Novell and Microsoft.

Even encryption codes are not completely secure. In September 1994, a hacker posted the encryption code for RSA, known as RC4, on Internet bulletin boards. Fortunately, damage may be minimal because having the code is not enough to compromise the system according to the code's owner.

An enhancement to encryption is a digital signature. A digital signature is an authentication technique in which the sender appends a coded identification to a message to ensure confidentiality. Only the authorized receiver can decipher the digital signature and thereby verify the sender's identity.

Microsoft and Visa are developing software that allows credit card holders to encrypt their card credit numbers for network transmission and use digital signatures to insure the integrity of transmitted information.

Biometric Devices

Your information may not need the full protection of sophisticated systems such as firewalls and encryption that can be expensive to obtain and time consuming to use. Yet since networks are only as strong as their weakest links, innovative security mechanisms are being introduced into the marketplace continuously.

An area where technology is simplifying our capability for verifying the identity of people using computing facilities is biometrics. Biometric devices are automated methods for validating a person's identity on the basis of such behavioral and physical characteristics as keystroke patterns, handwriting, voice patterns and fingerprints.

At an estimated price of $2,000 per point of identification, biometric devices are costly to implement. While biometrics may seem to us to be extreme measures now, they may not be so far-fetched in a world where schools install metal detectors at their entrances and universities require photo identification cards of students entering their cafeterias or libraries.

The lengths to which any organization will go to protect its information depend on the sensitivity of the information and the financial resources available. Steve Huber is manager of advanced technologies for Martin Marietta Information Systems in Orlando, Florida. He told me that biometric devices in use at Martin Marietta include retina scanning and facial and handprint imaging systems.[20] These technologies are sensitive enough to determine whether an unauthorized user is wearing a disguise such as a beard or wig.

The use of biometric devices will not replace the need for passwords, encryption and firewalls. Yet, it is important to keep in mind that biometric devices are emerging as a reliable method of automated personal identification in an increasingly automated environment.

Guidelines for the Development and Implementation of a Security Policy

The essence of the matter is that implementation of a security policy safeguarding your organizational resources is essential. A security policy reflecting your organization's mission, goals and objectives must be clearly delineated and rigorously administered.

There is no single solution for countering intrusions. Procedures for network security protection incorporated into your organization's security policy depend upon three factors:

- Information sensitivity.
- Mission critical applications.
- Your budget.

Brett Kemper said: "At the Broward County Library, we try to be cautious but we can't spend a million dollars protecting everything. We rely on security mechanisms built into our system and the good graces of our people."[21]

The goal of safeguarding an entire network against all incursions is unrealistic. A security policy indicates limits of acceptable behavior in the networked environment and defines responses to violations. Sanctions for failing to comply with security guidelines should be appropriate to infractions committed.

The security policy serves as a guide to the user community and acts as a deterrent to cyberinvaders. In creating a balanced security policy consistent with real world priorities, you should

- Identify computer network vulnerabilities through performing a risk analysis and security audit.
- Establish measures for reporting security breaches and reacting quickly when under attack.
- Specify tactics for backup to prevent catastrophe.
- Describe methods for disaster recovery.

Initial steps to take in developing an organizational security policy include

- Determining who is in charge of protection.
- Indicating network operations that are and are not allowable.
- Identifying resources susceptible to attacks.
- Establishing a security budget.
- Inventorying network security mechanisms.
- Forecasting the need for additional security devices.

Security education for all users is essential. Network changes should be reflected in modifications to the security policy. In order to maintain information confidentiality, restrict data access and prohibit data alteration, the security policy should be reviewed regularly and updated periodically.

Whether implementation of security safeguards is baseline or large-scale, we must become informed consumers in order to develop a security policy that accommodates current and projected requirements.

The problem of security has generated a multiplicity of service providers and claims of vendor and product superiority. Dr. Jane Anne Hannigan, professor emerita at Columbia University, advises: "We must carefully track advances in this domain so that we can deploy security solutions without being subjected to the pressure and flimflam artistry of vendors trying to dazzle us into making unwarranted acquisitions."[22]

Dr. Hannigan told me that a good approach is to create a watching brief or an annotated file of information that tracks the seemingly endless flow of innovative technology and service offerings. This brief can be kept on a World Wide Web home page, in an online directory or in diary format in a desk drawer.

One major aid to those instituting security policies and procedures is CERT. An acronym for the Computer Emergency Response Team, CERT was created as a response to a worm attack on the Internet that resulted in millions of dollars in lost productivity. The role of CERT is to identify and repair security breaches and transmit security related information to the Internet community. Individuals involved in network security can place their names on the CERT mailing list by sending an e-mail message to *cert-advisory-request@cert.org*. Security emergencies and suspicious network activities can be reported by calling the CERT 24-hour hotline at (412) 268-7090. Messages sent to CERT via e-mail to *cert@cert.org* concerning security intrusions should be encrypted.

The role of a librarian in the security arena can be as basic as making users aware of security guidelines at a computer terminal or as complex as designing a comprehensive security policy. Professional personnel with security-related responsibilities should become familiar with security technology in order to resolve security problems; recommend and develop procedures for safeguarding computer hardware, software and electronic information resources; and help build secure systems.

Conclusion

A variety of approaches can be used to design a network security policy. As we have seen, no network is totally protected against a cyber-hacker intent on exploiting it. Network security is complex. The Internet's rapidly expanding user population, information volume and application diversity continue to trigger difficult problems in the network security arena.

Safeguarding a network in the library environment involves constant vigilance and multiple approaches. Mechanisms such as passwords, encryption, firewalls and biometric devices are tactics that can be used to prevent destruction of network assets and interruption of library services. A watching brief is critical for tracking new security developments.

Computer security is a constant race between those who want to corrupt our networks and those who seek to protect them. Diligent security efforts can help us realize the benefits of internetworking while minimizing the destructive impact of cyberinvasions.

References

1. Eddie Williams, director of systems and administrative services, University Libraries, University of Southern Mississippi, personal communication, 14 January 1995.

2. Dr. B.R. Black, director of information technology of the Polk County (Florida) School System, personal communication, 15 March 1995.

3. Greg Rivera, Jr., systems librarian, Tampa Bay Library System Consortium, personal communication, 15 February 1995.

4. Maryln Kemper Littman, "The Perils of Network Security," in *Proceedings of the Sixteenth National Online Meeting*, ed. M.E. Williams (Medford, NJ: Learned Information, in press).

5. Alan Liddle, lieutenant commander, Royal Navy, and professor of systems management, National Defense University, personal communication, 20 January 1995.

6. Dr. Susan Anderson, library director, St. Petersburg Junior College, personal communication, 12 January 1995.

7. USAF Major William F. Conroy III, system software engineer, Global Transportation Network Program Management Office, United States Transportation Command, personal communication, 13 January 1995.

8. Brett Kemper, head of automated systems, Broward County Library, personal communication, 13 January 1995.

9. Dr. John Scigliano, vice president, computer and information technology, Nova Southeastern University, personal communication, 4 October 1994.

10. Greg Horne, manager of academic computing and strategic technologies, Nova Southeastern University, personal communication, 29 March 1995.

11. See note 5 above.

12. Dr. Jeanine Gendron, technology specialist, Coconut Creek High School, Coconut Creek, Florida, personal communication, 16 March 1995.

13. Donald Hyatt, director, computer systems lab, Thomas Jefferson High School for Science and Technology, Alexandria, Virginia, personal communication, 15 March 1995.

14. See note 8 above.

15. See note 5 above.

16. W.R. Cheswick and S.M. Bellovin, *Firewalls and Internet Security: Repelling the Wily Hacker* (Reading, MA: Addison-Wesley, 1994).

17. See note 9 above.

18. Dr. William Piotrowski, chief of information services, Leon County (Florida) School Board, personal communication, 5 March 1995.

19. James Litchko, director of business development for Trusted Information Systems, Inc., personal communication, 24 January 1995.

20. Steve Huber, manager of advanced technologies, Martin Marietta Information Systems, personal communication, 3 March 1995.

21. See note 8 above.

22. Dr. Jane Anne Hannigan, professor emerita, Columbia University, personal communication, 7 March 1995.

A Balancing Act: Copyright in the Electronic Network Environment

Laura G. Lape[1]

Trademarks can be infringed via electronic networks,[2] trade secrets may be misappropriated where, for example, a computer program is transmitted over a network, but the greatest intellectual property limitation on the flow of material and therefore information over electronic networks is copyright law. Recently the application of copyright law to electronic networks has been generating a great deal of discussion. The draft report of the Working Group on Intellectual Property Rights, a subgroup of the administration's Information Infrastructure Task Force, was issued last July, and has stimulated further controversy.[3] The final report, which I have been informed by the Patent Office should be out in May, will be a significant document in the ongoing process of determining how copyright fits into the electronic network environment.[4]

I will address the topic of copyright in the network environment from several perspectives: first, from the perspective of the policies that underlie copyright law; next, from the angle of one copyright doctrine, fixation, as it applies to networks; and last, from the viewpoint of the public interest in access to works, as that interest is served by doctrines such as fair use.

Copyright Policy and Distortions

Copyright law was not handed down with the Ten Commandments. From its beginning, and consistently through its history, the law of copyright has seen itself, not as natural law, handed down from on high, but as a tool, a means to an end. This is evident from the Copyright Clause of the Constitution, which is regularly cited in discussions of the theoretical basis of copyright law. The Copyright clause provides that Congress has the power to legislate in the area of copyrights in order to "promote the progress of science,"[5] or, to use twentieth century language, the progress of human knowledge. This conception of copyright law as a tool to achieve certain ends is apparent in court decisions, which frequently recite that copyright is not an end in itself, and that the reward of copyright protection is offered in order to serve a larger purpose.[6] Note, then, that copyright has not been traditionally seen from a natural law perspective, as a preexisting right, which the law simply protects.[7] Nor has it been justified on the same basis as continental *droit moral*, as protection to which a creator is entitled, simply because he has created.[8]

Rather, copyright has been seen as a way to promote the progress of knowledge, primarily by serving two policies: copyright protection is offered as an incentive to creators to create and to assure that the public has access to works.[9] These two policy concerns, incentive and access, are in tension with each other. To the extent that protection is tightened, there is less public access. To the extent that public access is increased, there is less protection. This incentive is provided in the Copyright Act by granting the creator of works the exclusive rights to reproduce the work, to make derivative works based on the work, to distribute the work publicly.[10] Public access to works is provided by the idea/expression dichotomy,[11] the fair use doctrine,[12] the first sale doctrine,[13] and by a host of additional exceptions such as the exemptions for libraries,[14] the small business exemption for performance of musical works,[15] the compulsory license for covering musical works, and the exemption for making necessary and archival copies of computer programs.[16] Access is thus a broad term, covering many different types of availability. Can you lift the ideas and information from a work and use them in a later work? Can you photocopy or quote or play over the radio someone else's expression? Can you just get your hands on a work, as where you borrow a book from a library or a friend, or rent a video? All of these questions fall under the rubric of access.

Recent discussions in high places of copyright and the information superhighway have distorted the classic balance of the copyright policy objectives, incentive and access. The result has been that proposals for accommodations of copyright law to the electronic network environment have been based on erroneous premises. Most significantly the draft report of the Working Group on Intellectual Property Rights distorts the traditional balance of policy objectives. The report tells us that intellectual property law must "(1) recognize the legitimate rights and commercial expectations of persons and entities whose works are used in the NII environment, and (2) ensure that users have access to the broadest feasible variety of works on terms and conditions that ... 'promote the progress of science'."[17] The distortion is in the first of these two objectives, where the draft report does not even mention the reason for providing copyright protection, that is, as an incentive for the creation of new works. Instead the report uses natural rights language, implying that all the law is doing is recognizing preexisting rights. The significance of this natural rights slant is that if the rights of creators are preexisting, then copyright law should impinge on these rights as little as possible. These are *rights*, after all, a word resonant in our society with all that is most sacrosanct.[18] If, on the other hand, as has traditionally been the case, copyright protection is a mere means to an end, which functions by offering an incentive for the production of new works, then we need offer only so much protection as is necessary to provide sufficient incentive. The natural rights approach biases the Working Group in the direction of overprotection, ignoring that Congress is authorized to adopt copyright protection only as a means to the end of promoting the progress of knowledge.[19]

The Working Group on Intellectual Property Rights is not alone in this misconstruction of the policy basis for copyright law.[20] The statement on fair use in the electronic age approved by the American Library Association at its midwinter conference similarly presents the balance as one between "the intellectual property interests of authors, publishers and copyright owners" and "society's need for the free exchange of ideas."[21] However, the balance under copyright doctrine is between the *public's* need for sufficient incentive and the public's need for access. Note that the public's need stands on both sides of the balance. The grant of rights to individuals is merely a means to an end.

The upshot of all this is that recent discussions of copyright and electronic networks have been skewed in the direction of protection at the expense of access. For example, the draft report of the Working Group presents detailed recommendations for the expansion and solidification of protections for copyright owners, such as the clarification of the distribution right by transmission and the creation of legal protection for anticopying systems, while promising that fair use and other guarantees of access such as the library exemptions will be dealt with later.[22] Indeed, as has been pointed out by Pamela Samuelson, the Working Group's misrepresentation of the current state of fair use law, if imposed as law, would greatly restrict the scope of that doctrine.[23] What apparent attention to access was given by the Working Group was in reality attention to protection in disguise. For example, the Working Group argued in favor of legal protection for anticopying systems on the ground that the "public will ... have access to more works" if such devices are protected because creators will have more incentive to produce.[24]

One final point needs to be made with respect to the incentive/access balance. There is a prevalent belief that every incremental increase in copyright protection will result in an incremental increase in the incentive to create. This assumption underlies the Working Group's draft report,[25] although it is an assumption whose truth has yet to be demonstrated, or even adequately addressed. In reality, it may well be that once a certain level of protection has been granted, incentive sufficient for our needs, or maybe even full incentive, has been offered. Indeed, it has even been argued, most notably by now Justice Breyer, that it is entirely possible that copyright protection is completely unnecessary as an incentive for the creation of works, and that other mechanisms, such as lead time, would provide adequate incentive.[26] Although I am not prepared to go that far and advocate abolishing copyright protection, we should not assume a direct relation between the degree of protection and the incentive to produce. Jessica Litman has pointed out that various exceptions to copyright protection that now exist have not discouraged creative activity.[27] For instance, the motion picture industry continues to prosper in spite of the first sale doctrine, which permits videotape rental businesses to rent videotapes.[28] Thus it is a mistake to assume that every increase in copyright protection will increase incentive and therefore benefit the public, producing weight in the balance between the public's need for sufficient incentive to create and the public's need for access.

The Fixation with Fixation

We turn now to the brass tacks of copyright in its relation to the information infrastructure. Due to the physical properties of electronic networks, many current discussions of copyright in this context turn on the definition of fixation under the Copyright Act.[29] Why the fixation with fixation? Fixation is defined as any embodiment of a work in a tangible object such that the work can be seen or otherwise communicated, either with a machine or without, for longer than a transitory period of time.[30] Therefore, where a work is stored in a computer for any length of time, as where material sent over the Internet is stored in a hard drive or on a disk or in the random access memory of the recipient's computer, we do have a fixation satisfying the current statutory definition.[31] This is embodiment in something tangible, which can be seen or communicated for more than a transitory period of time. It is not a "purely evanescent or transient" event, such as live television or "momentar[y]" capture in the memory of a computer, which were excluded from the realm of fixation by the legislative history of the 1976 Copyright Act.[32] Of course, any storage in a computer that is merely momentary will not satisfy the definition of fixation.[33]

Fixation has implications in copyright law for the answers to three questions: 1) Has a protectable work been created?; 2) Has the work been published?; and 3) Has the work been infringed?

First, fixation is a requirement for the creation of a protectable work.[34] Thus, where material is initially composed over an electronic network, so long as the material spends more than a brief period of time someplace along the way, such as storage on disk by a server or storage in the recipient's computer, assuming that the material is original and acceptable subject matter, a protectable work has been created.[35] Thus, the common assumption among users that material composed over the Internet is not subject to copyright protection is not, at least under current law, accurate.[36] Note that it is important to distinguish between the existence of copyright protection and the possibility that a contributor may, depending on the circumstances, have by implication licensed certain further uses of her material, such as forwarding the material to others.[37] But this does not mean that the material is not subject to copyright.[38]

The second implication of fixation is that publication occurs only where copies, that is, material objects in which the work is fixed, are distributed to the public by or under the authority of the copyright owner.[39] Therefore, where the copyright owner transmits a work such that a fixation of the work occurs in the computer of at least some members of the public, publication of that work has occurred.[40] The recommendation of the Working Group's draft report that the definition of publication in the act be amended to include the words "or by transmission," thus clarifies that publication can occur as a result of a transmission.[41] There are various consequences which follow under the Copyright Act from the publication of a work, not the least of which is that use of a published work is more likely to be fair use than use of an unpublished work.[42]

Third, and this is where the most attention has thus far been focused, fixation has implications for infringement. Two of the five ways to directly infringe a copyright require the existence of a copy: reproduction of copies and distribution of copies.[43] This means that where someone without authorization of the copyright owner causes a new copy, that is, fixation, of the work to be made in a computer by means of a network transmission, so long as no statutory exemption applies, and so long as the judicial test for infringement is met, the reproduction right has been infringed.[44] Further, where an unauthorized copy results from a transmission to the public, as over a digital network, even under current law, this appears to be a distribution within the meaning of the Act.[45] Again, so long as no statutory exemption applies, and so long as the judicial test for infringement is met, we have infringement. A single physical object did not pass from hand to hand, but the Act does not require that a single physical object pass from hand to hand.[46] Before the transmission, the recipient has no copy; after the transmission, the recipient has a copy. Thus, the amendment proposed by the Working Group's draft paper to add the words "or by transmission" to the list of ways that distribution can occur appears to merely clarify this point.[47] Not all commentators agree with the analysis of infringement I have just presented, although those few courts that have addressed the issue do agree.[48]

There are several points to bear in mind in considering this analysis of infringement. First, note that the Working Group's draft paper's proposed amendment would not make every transmission by any means whatever a distribution. Only those transmissions that result in a copy, on for example, a disk held by a server, create distribution. It is not the case that every transmission, for example, now by television, or by any means to be developed would be a distribution.

Secondly, if a transmission over a digital network did not create a fixation for infringement purposes, then it would also not create a fixation for the purposes of copyrightability and publication. This would mean that works initially created over the network would lack copyright protection, and that works originally created elsewhere would be unpublished if their only distribution were over the network, making fair use of these works somewhat less likely.

The third point to bear in mind is that quite aside from infringement by reproduction and distribution, transmission over a digital network, if to the public, and if of a work covered by the public performance right, such as a movie, or of a work covered by the public display right, such as a book or picture, would be an infringing performance or display.[49] Note that this would only be the case where no statutory exemption applied and if the judicial infringement test were met.[50] Thus, a given digital transmission of a movie, for example, might infringe the reproduction, distribution, *and* performance rights.[51] This means that copyright owners can control many transmissions by means of rights other than the reproduction and distribution rights.

Finally, we must clarify who bears the liability for any infringing transmissions. Concern has been expressed that the recipient of transmissions may be held liable for infringement by reproduction when a work is transmitted, due to the copy made in the recipient's computer.[52] The Working Group's draft report appears to contemplate just such a result. The draft report states that "when a computer user simply 'browses' a document resident on another computer, the image on the user's screen exists...only by virtue of the copy that has been reproduced in the user's computer memory" and that infringement results "whenever a digitized file is 'downloaded' from a BBS or other server."[53] While it is true that there may be infringement, the implication that the liability is the recipient's is a misconstruction of current law. Currently, for example, purchasers of infringing material are not held liable as contributory infringers.[54] They could not be held liable as direct infringers since they have not reproduced, made a derivative work, distributed, performed or displayed the work.[55] However, they arguably could be held liable as contributory infringers since their purchases do encourage the conduct of infringing distributors. However, copyright laws has not held such purchasers liable as contributory infringers.[56] By analogy, then, the infringing distributor over the digital network would bear the liability for any reproduction, distribution, and performance or display. The recipient would have no infringement liability.[57]

On the same topic, the statement on fair use in the electronic age of the American Library Association appears to state that liability for reception of transmissions should be dealt with as fair use.[58] This is both unwise and unnecessary. Fair use is always determined on a case by case basis and depends largely on the public utility of the particular use at issue.[59] The public's power to read or browse is far too important to be dependent on such rationales. Instead, under existing doctrine, as I have explained, receiving transmissions, and therefore reading and browsing, re not infringing acts, and therefore there is no need to resort to the defense of fair use.[60]

I would like to address briefly here the question which has been raised by some whether copyright is adequate to deal with the network environment, or whether we need some entirely new form of intellectual property protection in this context.[61] The suggestion has been that some new intellectual property regime is needed due to the differences between other media and electronic networks. These differences include the interactivity of networks and the relatively low cost to enter them, making it possible, for example, to infringe on a grand scale with little investment.[62] My conclusion, and I hope I am not overly influenced by my vested interest in copyright law, is that an entirely new form of protection is not needed.[63] I feel sure that the mere nature of the fixation over electronic networks does not necessitate abandoning copyright. The fixation rules transfer to this new medium relatively easily and continue to make theoretical sense in this new context. Fixation is merely a rough gauge of future availability. We reward a creator only when the work has been recorded in such a way that someone else is likely to have a chance to see it in the future. Publication depends on fixation because a creator who has distributed copies has made it more likely that at some future date a member of the public will be able to refer to the work or pass it on to someone else. And two types of infringement depend on fixation because by these acts the infringer has created or disbursed the work in a form that will permit others to use it later without recourse to the copyright owner. Fixation over electronic networks for creation, publication and infringement satisfies these rationales.

Fair Use

All may be fair in love and war, but there is some concern that little may be fair use over electronic networks. Fair use is a copyright doctrine that permits otherwise infringing uses, based largely on the benefit to society of permitting the unauthorized use.[64] For example, in various cases fair use has permitted making photocopies of an editorial from a newspaper and mailing them to various public officials,[65] including in a book on the assassination of President Kennedy copies of frames from the Zapruder film of the event,[66] making photocopies of scientific journals for medical research,[67] using VCRs to record television broadcasts for home viewing at a later time,[68] copying a computer program in order to discover how it worked,[69] and making and marketing a parody of a popular song.[70] Under our copyright system fair use is one of the major guarantors of access, making it possible for the expressive content of works to be copied without regard to permission from the copyright owner.

There is concern on the part of, among others, legal scholars and libraries that the scope of fair use on electronic networks may be constricted, particularly in light of the draft report of the Working Group on Intellectual Property.[71] The statement of the American Library Association on fair use in the electronic age argues that "as more information becomes available only in electronic formats,...the public's right of fair use must continue."[72] Certainly, if the Working Group's representation of the current scope of fair use were in fact the law, this important mechanism for providing access to works would be greatly restricted. For example, the Working Group states that the Supreme Court has created a presumption that all commercial uses are unfair, in spite of the fact that the Supreme Court had clarified in *Campbell v. Acuff-Rose Music, Inc.* that this is not the case.[73] In addition, the draft report misrepresents the significance of the Guidelines for Classroom Copying which were incorporated in the legislative history of the 1976 Copyright Act.[74] The Working Group's draft report states that "for the most part, educational fair use is limited to the type of copying expressly authorized in the 'classroom guidelines.'"[75] This was not the intention of the parties that negotiated the guidelines, nor was it the intention of Congress.[76] The guidelines were intended to be a safe harbor, that is, a description of uses that teachers could make with confidence that the uses were fair use. Other uses beyond the guidelines would also be fair use; the only difference is that a teacher making a use beyond the guidelines cannot have the same degree of certainty that the use is fair use. These misrepresentations of the state of current fair use law are an attempt to rewrite history in favor of incentive and against access.

The access currently provided by fair use and other access-promoting exemptions is also threatened by an amendment proposed by the Working Group to prohibit the manufacture or distribution of devices that defeat anti-use systems.[77] Technology can protect copyrighted works, but other technology can also defeat that protection. To deal with this perceived problem, the Working Group recommended making it copyright infringement to manufacture or distribute devices that defeat anti-copying systems. Note that under that language proposed by the Working Group, a suing copyright owner would not necessarily have to show that any work had been infringed using the device in order to prevail.[78] Systems or devices that prevent use of works by reproduction, distribution, performance or display would thus provide absolute protection because the devices needed to circumvent them would not be available. The Working Group's proposal thus ignores the many provisions under the Act for non-infringing use, such as fair use, certain copying by libraries, certain educational performances and displays, and archival copying of computer programs.[79] With absolute protection provided by anti-use systems, even where a given use would be fair use, for example, it could not be made.[80] Thus, for instance, a library entitled under current law to make a copy of a digital work for a patron, would be physically unable to do so.[81]

Finally, I want to address another threat to the access provided by fair use, this time a doctrine developed by the courts, known as productive or transformative use. This doctrine has significant implications for fair use over electronic networks because it provides that a use is less likely to be fair where a work is copied or otherwise used without alteration.[82] The significance for electronic networks is that a great deal of the copying or other use over networks which might be claimed to be fair use is nonproductive copying, that is copying of all or a portion of a work without making changes to produce a new work. Forwarding a work, for example, via e-mail to a friend is a nonproductive use. A doctrine of relatively recent vintage, productive use was first applied in the Ninth Circuit's decision in 1981 in *Universal City Studios, Inc. v. Sony Corp. of America*, a decision in which the court found that off-the-air home videorecording was not productive and therefore not a fair use.[83] The Supreme Court's reversal in *Sony* gave productive use little attention and argued against its significance in determining fair use.[84] However, the Supreme Court's enthusiastic and unanimous approval of the productive use doctrine in *Campbell v. Acuff-Rose Music, Inc.* in 1994 means that we are likely to see much more of this doctrine in the future.[85]

The productive use doctrine thus joins what has been in the last decade a series of judicial attempts to narrow the scope of fair use. We have seen the near exclusion of unpublished works from the scope of fair use, overruled by an amendment to the Copyright Act in 1992.[86] We have seen a growing exclusion of commercial uses from fair use, corrected by the Supreme Court in *Acuff-Rose*.[87] Now we have another wave in the attempt to limit fair use. Productive use is inconsistent with the fair use provision of the Act as adopted by Congress and with copyright doctrine as applied by the courts.[88] Further, by restricting fair use, the productive use doctrine shifts the balance between incentive and access, in favor of incentive and against access.

Conclusion

Where does all of this leave us? I think it leaves us, particularly those of us responsible for creating and applying copyright law, with some significant challenges. There may be attempts to impose copyright infringement liability on the recipient of transmissions. There certainly will be attempts to narrow the reach of access-providing doctrines such as fair use. And in discussions of copyright in the network environment, one danger is already a reality. That is the danger of losing sight of the fact that copyright is not a god-given right, but a tool we use to help motivate the creation of works so that the information in them will be available to our society. Only when seen properly, as a means to an end, will the rights granted by the Copyright Act be given appropriate weight in the balance between the public's need for sufficient incentive to create and the public's need for access.

References

1. Copyright, Laura G. Lape, 1995.
2. *Sega Enters., Ltd., v. Maphia*, 857 F. Supp. 679, 688 (N.D. Cal. 1994) (granting preliminary injunction based in part on likelihood of success on the merits of trademark infringement by use of trademark on programs made available for downloading from defendant's bulletin board); *Playboy Enters., Inc., v. Frena*, 839 F. Supp. 1552, 1561 (M.D. Fla. 1993) (finding that bulletin board service operator infringed plaintiff's trademarks).
3. *A Preliminary Draft of the Report of the Working Group on Intellectual Property Rights*, Information Infrastructure Task Force (July 1994) [hereinafter Draft Report].
4. Telephone conversation with Michael O'Neil of the Patent and Trademark Office (April 4, 1995) (stating that the final report is expected sometime in May of 1995).
5. U.S. Const. art. I, § 8. cl. 8.
6. *E.g., Fogerty v. Fantasy, Inc.*, 114 S. Ct. 1023, 1029 (1994) (stating that the copyright monopoly is "'intended to motivate the creative activity of authors ... by the provision of a special reward'"; *Sony Corp. of America v. Universal City Studios,* 464 U.S. 417, 429 (1984) (stating that the copyright monopoly "is intended to motivate the creative activity of authors"); *Twentieth Century Music Corp. v. Aiken,* 422 U.S. 151, 156 (1975) (stating that "the ultimate aim [of copyright law] is, by this incentive, to stimulate artistic creativity for the general public good"); *Mazer v. Stein,* 347 U.S. 201, 219 (1954) (stating that "[t]he economic philosophy behind the [copyright] clause ... is the conviction that encouragement of individual effort by personal gain is the best way to advance public welfare through the talents of authors").
7. For examples of natural rights doctrine see *Harbor View Improvement Assoc. v. Downey,* 311 A.2d 422, 425, 428 (Md. 1973) (affirming unenforceability of restrictive covenant and stating that "restrictions upon the use of land are in derogation of the natural right which an owner possesses to use and enjoy his property"); Richard A. Epstein, *Takings* 6, 85, 230–31 (1985) (stating that "trespass is not wrong because the state prohibits it; it is wrong because individuals own private property"; that "the rules of property uniquely specify the rights of all persons for all times"; that "there is some natural and unique set of entitlements that are protected under a system of private property").
8. Moral rights are generally defined as the right of paternity (the right to accurate attribution of works), the right of integrity (the right to be free from prejudicial modification of works), and the right to control publication of works. *See, e.g.*, Raymond Sarraute, *Current Theory on the Moral Right of Authors and Artists Under French Law*, 16 Am. J. Comp. L. 465, 480–81 (1968). Under the theory of continental droit moral, the creator is entitled to moral rights simply by virtue of having created, not in order to serve some further purpose.

9. The goal of promoting the flow of communication and the availability of works has been labeled access. *See, e.g., Fogerty v. Fantasy, Inc.,* 114 S. Ct. 1023, 1029, 1030 (1994) (stating that "private motivation [to create works] must ultimately serve the cause of promoting broad public availability of literature, music, and the other arts" and that "copyright law ultimately serves the purpose of enriching the general public through access to creative works"); *Feist Publications, Inc., v. Rural Tel. Servs. Co.,* 499 U.S. 340, 349–50 (1991) (stating that making ideas available "is the means by which copyright advances the progress of science and art").

10. 17 U.S.C. § 106 (1988).

11. 17 U.S.C. § 102 (b) (1988) (providing that "[i]n no case does copyright protection...extend to any idea, procedure, process, system, method of operation, concept, principle, or discovery"); *Feist Publications, Inc.,* 499 U.S. at 349–50 (stating that "copyright assures authors the right to their original expression, but encourages others to build upon the ideas and information conveyed by a work"); *Baker v. Selden,* 101 U.S. 99 104 (1879) (limiting the protection afforded to a book describing a system of bookkeeping by stating that the form of statement alone is protected by copyright).

12. *See* 17 U.S.C. § 107 (1988).

13. *See* 17 U.S.C. § 109 (a) (1988).

14. 17 U.S.C. § 108 (1988).

15. 17 U.S.C. § 110 (5) (1988).

16. 17 U.S.C. § 117 (1988).

17. Draft Report at 10.

18. *See* Mary Ann Glendon, *Rights Talk* 4–11, 20 (1991) (describing the American habit of speaking in terms of rights and criticizing the "exaggerated absoluteness of our American rights dialect").

19. The main focus of the Draft Report is, as set forth in the introduction to that report, that "information and entertainment products" may not be "protected effectively when disseminated via the NII." Draft Report at 6.

20. *See also* Lance Rose, *The Emperor's Clothes Still Fit Just Fine,* Wired, Feb. 1995, at 103 (asking "How can we balance efficiently the rights of multimedia developers to sample, alter, and incorporate older works against the rights of copyright owners to be paid whenever their works are used?).

21. Conference Proceedings, *Fair Use in the Electronic Age: Serving the Public Interest* 1 (Midwinter Conference of American Library Association, working document dated January 18, 1995). [see Appendix A]

22. The Working Group's draft report makes no specific recommendations to bolster fair use or other exceptions to copyright owners' exclusive rights, but announces a conference "to develop guidelines for fair uses of copyrighted works by and in public libraries and schools." Draft Report at 133. Compare the recommendations concerning distribution by transmission and protection of anti-copying systems. Draft Report at 120–130.

23. Pamela Samuelson, *The NII Intellectual Property Report* 37 Communications of the ACM 21, 24–25 (December, 1994); *see infra* notes 72–75 and accompanying text.

24. Draft Report at 125.

25. "[T]he potential of the NII will not be realized if the information and entertainment products protectable by intellectual property laws are not protected

effectively when disseminated via the NII. Owners of intellectual property rights will not be willing to put their interests at risk if appropriate systems ... are not in place to permit them to set and enforce the terms and conditions under which their works are made available in the NII environment." Draft Report at 6.

26. Stephen Breyer, *The Uneasy Case for Copyright: A Study of Copyright in Books, Photocopies, and Computer Programs*, 84 *Harv. L. Rev.* 281, 299–300 (1970) (stating that lead time and the threat of retaliation are advantages of the initial publisher that may offset a copier's lower production costs).

27. Jessica Litman, *The Exclusive Right to Read*, 13 Cardozo Arts & Entertainment L.J. 29, 46–48 (1994).

28. *Id.* at 46–47; 17 U.S.C. § 109(a) (1988).

29. 17 U.S.C. § 101 (1988).

30. 17 U.S.C. § 102 (a) (1988) (providing that "copyright protection subsists ... in original works of authorship fixed in any tangible medium of expression, now known or later developed, from which they can be perceived, reproduced, or otherwise communicated, either directly or with the aid of a machine or device"); 17 U.S.C. § 101 (providing that "a work is 'fixed' in a tangible medium of expression when its embodiment in a copy or phonorecord, by or under the authority of the author, is sufficiently permanent or stable to permit it to be perceived, reproduced, or otherwise communicated for a period of more than transitory duration").

31. *Vault Corp. v. Quaid Software, Ltd.*, 847 F.2d 255, 259 (stating that the 1976 Act established that "a program copied into a computer's memory constitutes a reproduction"); *Apple Computer, Inc., v. Franklin Computer Corp.*, 714 F.2d 1240, 1249 (3d Cir. 1983) (reaffirming that the requirement of fixation "is satisfied through the embodiment of the expression in the ROM devices"); *Williams Electronics, Inc., v. Artic Int'l, Inc.*, 685 F.2d 870, 874 (3d Cir. 1982) (finding that the memory devices of a videogame satisfy the requirement of a copy in which the work is fixed); Final Report of the National Commission on the New Technological Uses of Copyrighted Works, at 12 (1978) (stating that the "1976 Act ... makes it clear that the placement of any copyrighted work into a computer is the preparation of a copy").

32. H.R. Rep. No. 1476, 94th Cong., 2d Sess. 53 (1976), *reprinted in* 1976 U.S.C.C.A.N. 5659, 5666. "On the other hand, the definition of 'fixation' would exclude from the concept purely evanescent or transient reproductions such as those projected briefly on a screen, shown electronically on a television or other cathode ray tube, or captured momentarily in the 'memory' of a computer." *Id.*

33. *See, e.g., Advanced Computer Services of Michigan, Inc., v. Mai Systems Corp.*, 845 F Supp. 356, 363 (E.D. Va. 1994) (stating that "if a computer is turned off within seconds or fractions of a second of the loading, the resulting RAM representation of the program arguably would be too ephemeral to be considered "'fixed" or a 'copy' under the Act").

There is currently some controversy regarding whether storage in random access memory (RAM) satisfies the definition of fixation. Several recent cases have found that storage in RAM can be fixation. *Mai Systems Corp. v. Peak Computer, Inc.*, 991 F.2d 511, 519 (9th Cir. 1993) (holding in the context of infringement by reproduction that "the loading of software into the RAM creates a copy under the Copyright Act"); *Advanced Computer Services of Michigan, Inc., v. Mai Systems Corp.*, 845 F. Supp. 356, 363 (E.D. Va. 1994) (holding in the context of infringement by reproduction that "Where, as here, a copyrighted program is loaded into RAM and maintained there for minutes or longer, the RAM representation of the program is sufficiently 'fixed' to constitute a 'copy' under the Act"). Some commentators have argued that storage in RAM cannot be fixation within the meaning of the Copyright Act. Jessica Litman, *supra* note 27, at 42 (stating that "the act of reading a work into a computer's random access memory is too transitory to create a reproduction"); Pamela Samuelson, *supra* note 23, at 23 (arguing that storage in RAM is not fixation because by that logic holding a mirror up to a work would also be fixation).

34. U.S.C. § 102(a) (1988).

35. The Working Group's draft report shows confusion about the implications of simultaneous fixation for transmissions over the Internet. The report states that "works transmitted 'live' via the NII will not meet the fixation requirement, and will be unprotected by the Copyright Act unless the work is being fixed at the same time as it is being transmitted." Draft Report at 13. This is inaccurate. A work may achieve fixation by being recorded simultaneously with a transmission, but a later fixation will result in copyright protection, such protection beginning as soon as the work is fixed. 17 U.S.C. § 101 (1988) (stating that fixation can be made simultaneously with a transmission, but not stating that that is the only way that a transmitted work can be fixed).

36. For the proposition that users assume that material composed over the Internet is not protected by copyright, see Litman *supra* note 27, at 48, and Lance Rose, *Is Copyright Dead on the Net?*, Wired, Nov. 1993, at 112 (stating that some see the Net as "a collection of uncopyrightable discussions"). Contributors to lists rarely clarify their intentions regarding copyright, either by including a copyright notice or by including an express license regarding the future use of their material.

37. *See* Mark Lemley, Message to multiple recipients of list cni-copyright (March 31, 1995) (available from the author or from cni-copyright@cni.org) (stating that "the best approach is to say that you have impliedly licensed *certain types of copying* by placing your material on a publicly accessible Web page"). "Implicit—and in some instances explicit—protocols are also beginning to define reasonable e-mail practices and expectations." Deborah Reilly, *The National Information Infrastructure and Copyright: Intersections and Tensions,* 76 J. Pat. & Trademark Off. Soc'y 903, 919 (1994). Such expectations regarding the use others will make of material transmitted via networks could form the content of implied licenses to make such use.

38. The Working Group's draft report recommends amendment to the definition of publication and to the distribution right in § 106, but does not recommend any clarification of the definition of fixation for purposes of copyrightability. If the other two amendments are to be made, the definition of fixation for purposes of copyrightability should also be clarified by an amendment.

39. 17 U.S.C. § 101 (1988) (providing that "'[p]ublication' is the distribution of copies ... of a work to the public" and that "'[c]opies' are material objects ... in which a work is fixed by any method now known or later developed, and from which the work can be perceived, reproduced, or otherwise communicated, either directly or with the aid of a machine or device").

40. "Under the definition [of publication] in section 101, a work is 'published' if one or more copies or phonorecords embodying it are distributed to the

public—that is, generally to persons under no explicit or implicit restrictions with respect to disclosure of its contents—without regard to the manner in which the copies or phonorecords changed hands." H.R. Rep. No. 1476, 94th Cong., 2d Sess. 138 (1976), *reprinted in* 1976 U.S.C.C.A.N. 5659, 5754.

41. Draft Report at 123.

42. *Harper & Row, Publishers, Inc., v. Nation Enters.*, 471 U.S. 539, 564 (1985) (stating that "the scope of fair use is narrower with respect to unpublished works"). The last sentence of § 107 was adopted in 1992 to make clear that fair use of unpublished works is possible. An Act to Amend section 107 of title 17, Pub. L. No. 102-492, 106 Stat. 3145 (1992) (codified at 17 U.S.C. § 107 [1988]) (providing that "[t]he fact that a work is unpublished shall not itself bar a finding of fair use").

43. 17 U.S.C. § 106 (1), (2) (1988).

44. *See, Sega Enters., Ltd., v. Maphia,* 857 F. Supp. 679, 686-87 (N.D. Cal. 1994) (granting preliminary injunction against bulletin board operator based in part on finding of likelihood of success on the merits of direct and contributory infringement by making unauthorized copies of plaintiff's computer games both when games are uploaded onto the storage media of the bulletin board and when games are downloaded onto user's computers). For statutory exemptions, see for example 17 U.S.C. § 117 (1988) (permitting archival copies of computer programs and copies necessary for the utilization of the program), 17 U.S.C. § 108 (permitting libraries to make certain noncommercial copies), and 17 U.S.C. § 112 (permitting certain entities otherwise entitled to transmit to the public a performance or display of a work to make limited numbers of copies of certain works for temporary use). For the judicial test for infringement see *Arnstein v. Porter,* 154 F.2d 464, 468 (2d Cir. 1946) (stating that infringement requires "(a) that defendant copied from plaintiff's copyrighted work and (b) that the copying (assuming it to be proved) went so far as to constitute improper appropriation"), *Shaw v. Lindheim*, 908 F.2d 531, 534 (9th Cir. 1990) (stating that infringement requires substantial similarity of expression both objectively and subjectively), and Laura G. Lape, *The Metaphysics of the Law: Bringing Substantial Similarity Down to Earth, 98 Dickinson L. Rev.* 181, 182–83, 190–94 (1994) (explaining and criticizing the judicial test for infringement).

45. *Playboy Enters., Inc., v. Frena,* 839 F. Supp. 1552, 1556 (M.D. Fla. 1993) (finding that the right "to distribute copies to the public has been implicated by Defendant" BBS operator where subscribers uploaded plaintiff's photographs onto BBS; stating that "[t]here is no dispute that Defendant Frena supplied a product containing unauthorized copies of a copyrighted work"; finding infringement of the display right).

46. *See* 17 U.S.C. § 106(3) (1988) (providing that the copyright owner has the exclusive right "to distribute copies of the copyrighted work to the public by sale or other transfer of ownership, or by rental, lease or lending"); 17 U.S.C. § 501 (providing that whoever violates one of the exclusive rights of the copyright owner as provided by section 106 infringes).

47. The recommendation is to add the words "or by transmission" so that § 106 (3) would read "(3) to distribute copies or phonorecords of the copyrighted work to the public by sale or other transfer of ownership, or by rental, lease, or lending, or by transmission." Draft Report at 121.

48. *See, e.g.,* Pamela Samuelson, *supra* note 23, at 22 (stating that the report

"would give copyright owners an exclusive right to control digital transmissions of their works" and that this represents "another expansion" of current protection).

49. 17 U.S.C. § 106 (4), (5) (1988); 17 U.S.C. § 101 (1988) (defining 'to perform a work' as to render the work either directly or with a device and in the case of audiovisual works to show the images in any sequence; defining 'to display a work' as to show the images in any sequence; defining 'to display a work' as to show a copy of it, either directly or with a device; defining "to perform or display a work 'publicly'" as, *inter alia*, "to transmit or otherwise communicate a performance or display of the work…to the public, by means of any device or process, whether the members of the public capable of receiving the performance or display receive it in the same place or in separate places and at the same time or at different times"); *Playboy Enters., Inc., v. Frena*, 839 F. Supp. 1552, 1556 (M.D. Fla. 1993) (finding infringement of the public display right by transmission of photographs via defendant's bulletin board service).

50. For statutory exemptions to the public performance and public display rights, see 17 U.S.C. § 110 (1988). Certain of these exemptions for educational performances and displays may need to be expanded to cover educational reproductions and displays as the use of the NII in education becomes more important.

51. Thus, the last sentence in the Working Group's draft report's proposed definition of "to transmit," which was intended to distinguish between transmissions that are performances or displays and those that are distributions, is unnecessary. Draft Report at 122. An act of transmission could involve both a distribution and a performance or display. The Working Group appears to have assumed that a given act must be only one or the other, an unjustified assumption. The proposed test, "the primary purpose or effect of the transmission," is also unworkable, because it asks users and courts to determine the intent of those who made the transmission and whether the primary effect of the transmission was a performance or display on the one hand, or a distribution, on the other.

52. Litman, *supra* note 27, at 40; Samuelson, *supra*, note 23, at 22.

53. Draft Report at 35–37.

54. "Contributory infringement itself is of two types—personal conduct that forms part of or furthers the infringement and contribution of machinery or goods that provide the means to infringe." 3 Melville B. Nimmer & David Nimmer, Nimmer on Copyright, § 12.04[A], at 12–46 (1990). One who "with knowledge of the infringing conduct of another, may be held liable as a 'contributory infringer.'" *Gershwin Publishing Corp. v. Columbia Artists Management, Inc.*, 443 F.2d 1159, 1162 (2d Cir. 1971).

55. *See* 17 U.S.C. § 106 (1988).

56. *Cf. Demetriades v. Kaufmann*, 690 F. Supp. 289, 290, 296 (S.D.N.Y. 1988) (granting summary judgment on copyright infringement against purchasers of house to be built with infringing architectural plans where purchasers admitted they engaged in or were involved in the unauthorized copying of the plans).

57. The Working Group's draft report does hint that the doctrine of contributory infringement may have some relevance in resolving the issues discussed in the text. Draft Report at 36.

58. Conference Proceedings, *Fair Use in the Electronic Age: Serving the Public Interest* 2 (Midwinter Conference of American Library Association, working document dated January 18, 1995) (apparently stating that fair use should cover the power "to read, listen to, or view publicly marketed copyrighted material

privately, on site or remotely" and "to browse through publicly marketed copyrighted material"). [see Appendix A]

59. *Meeropol v. Nizer*, 417 F. Supp. 1201, 1207 (1976) (stating that in determining fair use "an extremely important consideration is the public interest served by the use of the copied materials"), *rev'd in part*, 560 F.2d 1061 (1977); *Williams & Wilkins Co. v. U.S.*, 487 F.2d 1345, 1354, 1356, 1359 (Ct. Cl. 1973) (relying on the social utility of medical science, which would be harmed if the photocopying at issue were stopped); Laura G. Lape, *Transforming Fair Use: The Productive Use Factor in Fair Use Doctrine*, 58 Albany L. Rev. 101, 139 (1995) (stating that the public utility of the use has traditionally been important in fair use determinations).

60. The doctrine of fair use is an affirmative defense which excuses an otherwise infringing use. 2 Paul Goldstein, Copyright § 10.1, at 187 (1989) (stating that "[c]ourts have for more than a century excused certain otherwise infringing uses of copyrighted works as 'fair' uses").

61. *E.g.*, Office of Technology Assessment of the U.S. Cong., Intellectual Property Rights in an Age of Electronics and Information 3 (1986) (stating that "the new information and communications technologies available today are challenging the intellectual property system in ways that may only be resolvable with substantial changes in the system or with new mechanisms to allocate both rights and rewards").

62. For the differences between bulletin board systems and older media, see Lance Rose & Jonathan Wallace, Syslaw 8 (1992).

63. *See id.* at 41 (stating that copyright, trademark, trade secrets and patent which "developed through many past changes of information technology, are quite adequate for defining property boundaries within current communications technology").

64. *See* 17 U.S.C. § 107 (1988); Laura G. Lape, *supra* note 59, at 118–120.

65. *New York Tribune, Inc., v. Otis & Co.* 39 F. Supp. 67, 68 (S.D.N.Y. 1941).

66. *Time, Inc., v. Bernard Geis Assocs.*, 293 F. Supp. 130, 145–46 (S.D.N.Y. 1968).

67. *Williams & Wilkins Co. v. United States,* 487 F.2d 1345, 1354, 1356, 1359 (Ct. Cl. 1973), *aff'd per curiam*, 420 U.S. 376 (1975).

68. *Sony Corp. of America v. Universal City Studios, Inc.,* 464 U.S. 417, 456 (1984).

69. *Sega Enters., Inc., v. Accolade, Inc.,* 977 F.2d 1510, 1518 (2d Cir. 1992).

70. *Campbell v. Acuff-Rose Music, Inc.,* 114 S. Ct. 1164, 1179 (1994).

71. *E.g.*, Samuelson, *supra* note 23, at 24 (stating that the Working Group's draft report "takes such a narrow view of existing fair use law and predicts such a dim future for fair use law when works are distributed via the NII that the report might as well recommend its abolition").

72. Conference Proceedings, *supra* note 58, at 1.

73. 114 S. Ct. 1164, 1173–74 (1994) (stating that the commerciality of the use has no "hard presumptive significance" and that commerciality merely "'tends to weigh against a finding of fair use'"; Draft Report at 48, 51. The origin of the supposed presumption that commercial uses are not fair use was a statement to that effect in the Supreme Court's decision in *Sony. Sony Corp. of America v. Universal City Studios,* 464 U.S. 417, 451 (1984). Justice Brennan in dissent in *Harper*

& *Row*, as well as lower court decisions, had pointed out that such a rule would make no sense and surely could not really have been intended by the Supreme Court. *Harper & Row, Publishers, Inc., v. Nation Enters.,* 471 U.S. 539, 592 (1985) (Brennan, J., dissenting). The Supreme Court in *Acuff-Rose* agreed. 114 S. Ct. at 1174 (stating that "if commerciality carried presumptive force against a finding of fairness, the presumption would swallow nearly all of the illustrative uses listed in the preamble paragraph of § 107, including news reporting, comment, criticism, teaching, scholarship, and research since these activities 'are generally conducted for profit'" and that "*Sony* itself called for no hard evidentiary presumption").

74. H.R. Rep. No. 1476, 94th Cong., 2d Sess. 67–70 (1976), *reprinted in* 1976 U.S.C.C.A.N. 5659, 5680–83.

75. Draft Report at 49.

76. "The purpose of the following guidelines is to state the minimum and not the maximum standards of educational fair use...the following statement of guidelines is not intended to limit the types of copying permitted under the standards of fair use under judicial decision and which are stated in Section 107. *Id.* at 68, *reprinted in* 1976 U.S.C.C.A.N. at 5681.

77. Draft Report at 126–27. The anti-use systems would be technological devices or systems that would prevent one or more of the uses specified by § 106: reproduction, distribution, public performance or display.

78. Draft Report at 127; Samuelson, *supra* note 23, at 25.

79. 17 U.S.C.§ § 107, 108, 110, 117 (1988). The proposed amendment is thus inconsistent with a decision by the Fifth Circuit that selling a program that defeated a copy-protection program was not contributory infringement because the former program permitted users to make archival copies of programs, as permitted by § 117(2). *Vault Corp. v. Quaid Software, Ltd.,* 847 F.2d 255, 267 (1988).

80. *See* Litman, *supra* note 27, at 32 n.21. "Devices that overcome technological copy-protection methods can have legitimate uses.... Copy protection devices can, after all, block access in situations when the copyright statute would privilege it." *Id.*

81. The Working Group's draft report defends its proposal on the grounds that "legislation of this type is not unprecedented" and cites § 1002, adopted in the Audio Home Recording Act of 1992, as an example. Draft Report at 126; Audio Home Recording Act of 1992, Pub. L. No. 102-563, 106 Stat. 4237 (codified at 17 U.S.C. § 1002 [1988]). There are, however, important distinctions between § 1002 and the draft report's proposal. Section 1002 (c) protects serial copy management systems, which are systems that prevent second generation digital audio copies, but permit first generation digital audio copies. 17 U.S.C. § 1002. Thus, serial copy management systems do not prevent all copying. Secondly, § 1002 was adopted as part of a negotiated package which also included § 1008, a new exemption from infringement liability, which provides that as of 1992 there is no infringement liability for manufacturing or distributing audio recording devices or media, or for making noncommercial home musical recordings. 17 U.S.C. § 1008 (1988). Therefore, an important concession to access was part of the trade-off for § 1002 (c). In the case of the Working Group's proposals, there is no such trade-off in favor of access.

The report seeks to further defend its proposal on the grounds that the proposed amendment prohibits the manufacture or distribution of devices that circumvent anti-use systems *except* where the law would permit deactivating the anti-use system. Draft Report at 127, 130. The Working Group appeared to be primarily concerned with works whose copyright term has expired and works otherwise in the public domain. Draft Report at 130. The report states that since devices can be distributed to circumvent anti-use systems where "the primary purpose or effect" is to deactivate systems protecting works unprotected by law, there would be no problem. Draft Report at 127, 130. However, will such deactivating devices be available, where their manufacturers would be liable under the Act if it could be shown that the "primary purpose *or effect*" of the deactivating device was to permit infringing use. If substantial infringing use resulted from the distribution of the deactivating device, the manufacturer would be liable.

    82. Productive or transformative use has been defined as use not for "any socially useful purpose," but as copying that "produce[s] something new and different from the original," that is, a new work. *American Geophysical Union v. Texaco, Inc.,* 802 F. Supp. 1, 11, 14 (S.D.N.Y. 1992), *aff'd,* 37 F.3d 881 (2d Cir. 1994).

    83. 659 F.2d 963, 970–72 (9th Cir. 1981), *rev'd,* 646 U.S. 417 (1984).

    84. *Sony Corp. of America v. Universal City Studios, Inc.,* 464 U.S. 417, 455 n.40 (1984).

    85. 114 S. Ct. 1164, 1171, 1173, 1176–77, 1179 (1994); *see American Geophysical Union v. Texaco, Inc.,* 37 F.3d 881, 890–91 (2d Cir. 1994) (citing *Acuff-Rose,* 114 S. Ct. at 1171-73) (arguing that the district court properly emphasized the issue of "transformative use" because after the district court opinion was issued, "The Supreme Court explicitly ruled that the concept of a 'transformative use' is central to a proper analysis under the first factor"); *Princeton University Press v. Michigan Document Servs., Inc.,* 855 F. Supp. 905, 909–910 (E.D. Mich. 1994) (decided after *Acuff-Rose* and relying in part on lack of productive use to find no fair use). For the development of the productive use doctrine, see Laura G. Lape, *supra* note 59, passim.

    The Working Group's draft report presents productive use, inaccurately, as a traditional tenet of fair use law. Draft Report at 46–47.

    86. The amendment to § 107 added the sentence: "The fact that a work is unpublished shall not itself bar a finding of fair use if such finding is based upon consideration of all the above factors." An Act to Amend section 107 of title 17, Pub. L. No. 102-492, 106 Stat. 3145 (1992) (codified at 17 U.S.C § 107 (1988). The amendment was intended to "overrule the overly restrictive language of *Salinger* and *New Era* with respect to the use of unpublished materials." S. Rep. No. 141, 102d Cong., 1st Sess. 5; *see Salinger v. Random House,* 811 F.2d 90 (2d Cir.), *cert. denied,* 484 U.S. 890 (1987); *New Era Publications Int'l v. Henry Holt & Co.,* 873 F.2d 576 (2d Cir. 1989), *cert. denied,* 493 U.S. 1094 (1990).

    87. *Campbell v. Acuff-Rose Music, Inc.,* 114 S. Ct. 1164, 1173–74; *see supra* note 73 for a discussion of commerciality in fair use.

    88. *See* Lape, *supra* note 59, at 138–48.

Freedom of Speech and Censorship in the Electronic Network Environment

Michael Godwin

I want to do a whirlwind tour of what I think the free speech and censorship issues are on the electronic frontier. I would have preferred "electronic frontier" rather than "electronic network environment" in the title of this talk, but since I'm a professional, I do have to use three words where other people would use two. I want to point out that what we're seeing here is something that is really new. Ecclesiastes says there is nothing new under the sun, but here there is something really new: A new medium that is different from all other media that have ever preceded it.

How is it different? We are all familiar with speech. Speech is basically a one-to-one medium that works best when we are face to face. It works least well when you have some guy standing in front of a room talking to people. Speech works best one to one: It is a two-way medium, people exchange information, it is very intimate, the information goes in multiple directions. But it is not normally very powerful in and of itself. You have to enhance it or change it in some way to make it powerful. The telephone gives you some distance for speech. You can use the telephone and talk long distance, but the telephone is essentially a one-to-one medium just as speech is. How do you know? Ever participate in a conference call? Nothing is more awkward and painful than a conference call, where you are trying to use a one-to-one medium as a group communications medium and it never works properly. You are talking and you are pausing, waiting for someone else to talk, and you're never quite sure when to jump in. There is always one party who is on a speaker phone, and someone is constantly being cut off. Every conference call I have ever participated in lasted approximately three to five times as long as the conversation would have taken if we had been in the same room.

Fortunately, human beings are inventive; we have developed other media that have different attributes. The press is one. The press has the ability to reach out to large audiences, and in fact that is what newspapers and books and magazines do. This ability comes at a certain price, because the two-way information flow that you're familiar with in speech and even sometimes in speaking situations like this symposium, isn't there, for the most part. There is not a lot of feedback from the audience to the centralized production of information in a one-to-many medium. Telephones are one to one, speech is one to one, but the press is one to many. And one-to-many communications media tend to be uni-directional. They send information, but not too much comes back. Television is very similar, right? The movies are very similar: one-to-many communications. You have highly centralized, highly capitalized communications media. You have to be rich, normally, in order to send your message through these media.

The information goes one way. There are some exceptions to this: "Dear Abby," the op-ed page, the letters to the editor page. But it is very hard to get into those. My favorite exception actually is "Ask Beth," where the same questions resurface over and over again: "He says, if I loved him..." So I am familiar with the attempts to make one-to-many communications a little more two-way, but for the most part, they are failures. Nothing is quite so painful as having submitted a letter to the editor and having had it edited for space. But this new medium, this online communication that we are now increasingly participating in, is something very different: It is many to many. Every person who is participating online is not just a consumer of information: He or she is a producer as well. So you have the same kind of two-way or multi-directional interactivity that you have in speech on the telephone, but you have translated it to a mass medium. Suddenly everybody can reach a large audience.

The example I always give comes from having been editor of *The Daily Texan*, and I often think of this when I post messages online. When I was an editor of this university newspaper, which was a daily with a circulation of about thirty-five thousand, we flattered ourselves that our pass-along readership added another ten or fifteen thousand. Those of you who have worked in newspaper advertising know what I mean. I was sitting on top of a million or a couple of million dollars' worth of physical plant in order to reach that audience. Suddenly we live in a world in which for a few hundred dollars any of us can reach many times that audience. This makes a fundamental difference because, for the first time since the founding of the Republic, the First Amendment becomes a right that is deeply personal, insofar as it protects press and speech interests.

If you think of the beginning of the United States, the people who were doing the printing and publishing were small entities for the most part, not multimedia huge conglomerates like Time-Warner or Gannett or Paramount. But not everybody was a publisher or a printer and most people weren't. So, for them the First Amendment was primarily a protection for speech. But now everybody is potentially a publisher or a printer. A.J. Liebling, a writer for *The New Yorker* and a famous sports writer, once commented that freedom of the press belongs to those who own one. We all potentially own one now, and that is changing the world in some fundamental ways. Because the world is changing in fundamental ways, it is really important that we take the protections that the First Amendment has long provided and make sure they apply to those of us who are little guys as well as to the big media defendants who normally cite the First Amendment, and who, when they do it, seem to be engaging in a form of special pleading. The First Amendment is up close and personal now, and I want to talk about some of the ways in which our First Amendment interests, which are now stronger than ever before, are also more threatened than ever before.

I am going to take a side road on this and step back and talk a little bit about the hype of the Internet. This is not news to you that the Internet has been hyped, right? Cliff Stoll, my friend, has written a book called *Silicon Snake Oil* (Doubleday, 1995). Cliff is a family man now. He's settled down and has had a child. It's hard for him, living everyday life, not to suddenly remember that there are pleasures about being human and in your body and out on the street that you really don't get by being cooped up in an artificially lit room facing a cathode ray tube. And so he talks about that. I think it is fair to say that his meditation on the hype surrounding the information superhighway is worth reading and raises important questions. But the fact that the Internet has been hyped doesn't mean that it's no good at all. Lots of good things were also overhyped—penicillin comes to mind.

Thinking about the Internet, however, we have to remember that this second wave of appraisal where we now look at the network communications and say they are not the greatest thing in the world after all, should not let us fall into reflexive regulation or censorship, simply because the Internet never will live up to all of those promises that it never could have lived up to. If you read the news coverage in 1993, the information superhighway was bringing us five hundred channels. We were told that everybody was going to be taking French courses from people in other countries—ideally France. We were told that medical information was going to be widely shared on the Net, improving our medical care. We were told that the Internet would be connected to every school. That last promise was troubling to many of us who spent time on the Internet because we had an idea of who and what was on the Internet and were not terribly sure that connecting every school was the best idea. What we now see is this notion that flames and pornographers are being used as the thin entering wedge of an attack on this medium. There is something about sex that enables policy makers to get headlines, to get votes, and to rant and rave at length in the halls of Congress and the halls of our state legislatures. We are not a society that is terribly comfortable with sex in spite of the fact that we have an incredibly deep interest in it. As a result, even though we now live in a world where I would say more than half of the people in the country are comfortable with the fact that there is a lot of sexual information out there—available on the Net, in libraries, and elsewhere—it is still easy to push our buttons by saying, "But what about the children?" You and I may not care what somebody views on his VCR in the privacy of his home, but what about the children?

You see that with Senator Exon's Communications Decency Act where he proposes taking the regulatory regime that we have had in broadcasting, making it worse, and then imposing it on network communications. I want us to step back and not reflexively regulate here, partly because I don't think that regulation is necessary and partly because I think it would be a tragedy if we did. The First Amendment protects so many interests that are implicated on the Net that the Internet and the communications like the Internet are really fundamentally the greatest experiment in freedom of expression that the globe has ever seen. It is amazing when we talk about compression in the computer context, nobody ever praises the compression of the First Amendment because there's a lot in there. Freedom of speech, freedom of the press, freedom of assembly, freedom to petition the government for a redress of grievances. I forgot for a long time that those were the fundamental First Amendment rights that were relevant to network communication, until one day I was reading news groups and I came across a debate between people who preferred the Macintosh to those who preferred the IBM PC, and I realized that free exercise of religion was also relevant.

Does the First Amendment apply in cyberspace? Five years ago that subject seemed to be open to debate. When the Electronic Frontier Foundation started saying that when you close bulletin-board systems (BBS's), you are affecting people's First Amendment rights, I heard some people like Gene Spafford at Purdue University ask whether the First Amendment applies in cyberspace. He said, "How do you know? You don't even know if this kind of communication is speech or the press or what." And I said, "Gene, you know the First Amendment protects both speech and the press, so I don't even have to answer the question." But he said, "How do you even know it's speech? Maybe it's just some kind of utterance. Maybe it's not even really speech." He sent me this in E-mail and I wrote back and I said, "Gene, I'm sorry. I can't understand the question. Please call me at this number." He understood the point.

I don't think today even Gene debates the applicability of the First Amendment. What he does debate and what other people debate is whether certain kinds of speech, now that we recognize it as speech, should be allowed on the Net. You have to recognize the fact that every time a new communications medium has been introduced, governments have been frightened by it and have stepped in and attempted to regulate it. This is without exception. The printing press was licensed in Great Britain and elsewhere, and in some countries it still is licensed. In Britain, a publisher had to print an extra copy for the censor to review and make sure it was acceptable. Of course, we learned a lot from the licensing of the press. When we started this country, we forbade the government to license the press. On the other hand, we licensed broadcasters, with an idea that because of the supposed scarcity of the broadcasting spectrum and because of the pervasiveness of broadcasting as a medium, it is appropriate for government to step in and protect us from broadcasters and from ourselves. I think that has been our experiment with the licensed press, and I think it has been a failed experiment. But of course, we are so used to having broadcasting regulated now that nobody even thinks about repealing the content control powers inherent in the FCC. The nicest thing that could be said about the FCC is that at least it is limited to broadcasting. Presumably, everything else is protected in a very strong sense by the First Amendment.

Looking at network communications, you see that the traditional justifications for the regulation of broadcasting aren't there. There is no scarcity of the resource; in fact, every time you add another computer to the Internet, you increase the size of the Internet. Scarcity is not a problem. Is it pervasive in the same sense that George Carlin's monologue on seven dirty words was pervasive when it came over the radio at WBAI in New York? I don't think so, because whereas broadcasting pushes information towards an audience, on the Net you pull information towards you. It is not the case that you log on and suddenly offensive and disturbing information floods over your screen. So, I think that we have to begin with the assumption and with the presumption that the First Amendment strongly protects Net communications and go from there. I think we are winning that fight at least so long as we prevent the passage of the Exon bill in its current form, which would put network communications under the FCC's rule-making authority.

But that is not the only fight. There are fights about obscenity. Many of you know about the case involving Robert and Carleen Thomas in Milpitas, California, who ran a bulletin-board system with adult material that billed itself as the dirtiest place on earth. Probably bad advertising, because some well-meaning postal inspectors in Memphis, Tennessee, decided to see if they could drag the dirtiest place on earth into court in Tennessee. Remember, Milpitas is in northern California, about thirty miles south of San Francisco. Many of you know that obscenity is defined based on community standards. In northern California, there are no "community standards" in some places. The Thomases were certain they were operating within the scope of the law in San Francisco, and they never anticipated that a postal inspector in Memphis would be so hot to drag them into court that he would call up and download images and create jurisdiction for them to be convicted in a U.S. district court in Memphis, Tennessee. That happened, and that case is now under appeal. It is hard to think about how you distinguish that case from a case in which someone in Memphis drove to California, bought something in a book store or an adult video store on Columbus Avenue in San Francisco and then drove back to Memphis. Remember, on the Net, you pull information. People aren't pushing it on you. It's very different from the broadcasting of obscenity.

There is another issue here, and that concerns the community-standards rationale as created in *Miller v. California*, with an idea of preventing the most liberal jurisdictions in the country from dictating standards for the most conservative ones. Chief Justice Warren Burger had the idea that it would be unfit for New York or Los Angeles or San Francisco to dictate the standards for Kansas City or for Memphis. Surely it is wrong to apply that same decision to let the most conservative jurisdictions in the country dictate the standards for the most liberal ones. That can't be right and that is one of the issues that is being raised in the appeal of the *United States v. Robert and Carleen Thomas*.

It's not just talk about sex, although that raises freedom of speech issues on the Net. We have a case recently about a University of Michigan student named Jake Baker who published a rape/murder fantasy on the Net in which he included as the name of a character the name of a woman who is actually a student at the University of Michigan. It is very hard to hear about this without feeling queasy, without feeling that there's something really troubling about that. I think it is very fair to say that he has pushed the envelope of what we ought to find acceptable.

Yet if you think as lawyers for a moment, you find that there are actually freedom of speech issues lurking behind the facts of this case. Strictly speaking, there are all sorts of ways that we can make speech a crime. Criminal conspiracy is one, but Baker does not seem to have conspired. Invasion of privacy is another but if you look at the invasion of privacy causes of action that the courts recognize, you find that he doesn't quite fit into any of those. Even the U.S. government found it difficult to find an excuse to indict him but, creatively, they took the federal threats statute, which criminalizes the interstate transmission of threats, and indicted him in what turns out to be a very unusual use of the statute, even though the story clearly was not intended as a threat. In fact, Baker published it and it appeared on the Net and nobody complained about it, not knowing that a real woman's name had been used. After a while, comment ended and it was only a month later when a University of Michigan alum in Moscow (what a world we live in!) read the story and, disturbed by its content— not by its use of anyone's name—called up the University of Michigan and tried to get the guy punished. Well, he succeeded.

I think what we will find in this case is what we find often when prosecutors are challenged to try to adapt current laws to the issues raised by the Net. You see them attempting to show that we can police the Internet and we can use laws creatively to do it. If you are a civil libertarian, however, whenever you see creative uses of criminal laws, you should pause and ask, what is the meaning here? Here we have a case where the prosecutors have forgotten what the First Amendment is about because the First Amendment is designed to protect offensive, troubling, disturbing speech. Nobody ever tries to ban the other kind. And because the First Amendment now is a personal right, this is a right that matters to all of us who participate in the Net, and all of us are going to find ourselves saying something that disturbs someone else. We can't avoid it. That's what human beings do. It is important that we not see government step in and start classifying speech as a new sort of crime.

Still another case—copyright infringement. We had a case in Boston involving an M.I.T. student named David LaMacchia. He had set up a bulletin-board system on the Internet which other people allegedly used to trade commercial copies of software. The government was very troubled by this and wanted to indict him for something. But it was very hard to fit his actions under the copyright act because criminal copyright provisions are limited to willful and commercial benefit. In fact, they indicted him for wire fraud because wire fraud is one of those big mushy federal statutes that can be made to fit all sorts of behavior so long as telephone use is involved. If the prosecutors had read the law of criminal copyright, they'd have discovered a case from 1985 in which the Supreme Court decided that when you have a criminal copyright infringement, you must stick to the Copyright Act. You don't get to use those big mushy general federal statutes. So you have a case almost ten years old that pretty much dictates the outcome in the LaMacchia case because LaMacchia's case was dismissed. Why did the prosecutors ignore that 1985 case? A couple of reasons. You can theorize that they are just dumb and that they just don't do their research. That's actually true with many prosecutors, it's true of many defense lawyers. I think what's more likely is that the prosecutors thought, there's just something very troubling about copyright infringement and we want to show that we're out there policing people's copyright interests. And if the cases don't support us, maybe we can get a judge to overturn the case. Maybe we can get a judge to distinguish our case from other cases. Maybe we can successfully prosecute this kid and even if our prosecution fails, we will have punished him because being federally indicted is punishment in and of itself. Those are some of the issues that show what happens when you have prosecutorial over-reaching.

I want to talk to you about privacy issues as well because I think they are relevant. There was a case in 1958 involving the National Association for the Advancement of Colored People in which a state government, Alabama, insisted on having the organization disclose its membership list. This was nominally under a statute to prevent Communist front organizations from operating in Alabama. As a practical matter, if you were living in Alabama in 1958, your membership in the N.A.A.C.P. may have been something you wanted to keep to yourself. And they knew that. The United States Supreme Court held in *N.A.A.C.P. v. Alabama* that your right to privacy is an interest that is guaranteed under the First Amendment because sometimes you need privacy to speak freely and to speak confidentially. The Supreme Court has consistently upheld that and most recently upheld it this week (of April 16, 1995) in a case involving anonymous distribution of political flyers. The Court recognized the value of anonymity. And yet some people see the growth of anonymous free mailers on the Net as something inherently threatening. They devise nightmare scenarios in which people use anonymous free mailers to distribute copyrighted material or trade-secret material and somehow kick the legs out from under the American intellectual property industry. I think that, once again, you have to step back from the fear mongers and say, look, isn't this really just a reflexive caution about a new medium, the same kind that we always see whenever a new medium is created? Is there really a problem here or are you just anticipating one?

There is one other issue I think that ought to be raised. It is related to anonymity and involves encryption. Our government is very, very troubled by the prospect that we can decide to keep something a secret and mean it. The technology of encrypting material so that even the N.S.A. (National Security Administration) can't read it turns out to be cheap and easily available and runs on any computer you can buy in any store today. You can't export it. The government has also declared it a munition. In spite of that, foreign governments and foreign individuals have access to encryption but not in a way that creates any benefit for American software companies because we can't sell it over there. The government says that if you would make encryption commonplace, then our valued interest in wire tapping is undermined. Don't laugh! They say wire tapping is serious business and believe me, if a government representative were here speaking now, the first thing they would do is cite the explosion in Oklahoma: What if a successful wire tap could have prevented that bombing? Are you so sure you want encryption? How valuable is your privacy? What if we could have prevented that Oklahoma bombing? (a year or two ago it was the World Trade Center). I have to say that that is exactly the kind of argument you're going to see against encryption.

Right now the government is attempting to promote encryption schemes that require that the keys be kept by government agencies. This seems like requiring that a copy of the key to your house be kept at the police department in case they ever have to do a search and seizure. They don't like it when I compare it to that. They'll talk about terrorism, maybe even nuclear terrorism, they'll talk about organized crime, they'll talk about drug cartels and they'll say, weighed against our interests in policing these threats to society, how valuable, really, is your need to keep your communications private? The only thing I can say in response to that is that this government was founded on the idea that citizens' and individual rights were the primary rights and that government was a tool for us. We were not a tool for it. The United States was grounded and organized on a fundamental distrust of government and government purposes, a distrust that the framers of the Constitution found entirely relevant to their everyday lives and one not hard for us to find relevant in our lives. Even conservatives and liberals can unite on the issue of distrust of government power.

There is one final attack on the First Amendment that you are going to see and that is one that I have seen most recently from Gary Chapman, who used to be head of Computer Professionals for Social Responsibility and now heads the Twenty-first Century Project at the University of Texas. He has this idea that the First Amendment was designed primarily to protect serious political speech and so all this flaming and talk about sex and other nasty stuff on the Net isn't worth protecting. In other words, we think the First Amendment is a great thing, but we never thought all these people would be using it so irresponsibly.

I have to say that the irresponsible use of speech is not only protected by the First Amendment but it is a fundamental human interest. We were designed to talk to each other and when we talk to each other, we are frivolous, we make jokes, we play, we play with words. Look at something like a sonnet, which is not political speech in any way, shape or form— should this be protected by the First Amendment? I hope it should. I would be astonished if it was not.

This is the first time in history that the power of a mass medium is in the hands of individuals. Potentially, everybody has this immense opportunity to participate in the greatest experiment in freedom of speech and in democratic communication that the world has ever seen. If I could leave you with one thought, I would say that it is up to you now to protect this opportunity, to exploit it, and not to lose it.

Discussion

Mary K. Chelton, Rutgers Ph.D. candidate (to Godwin): You passed very quickly over, "What about the children?" When I was at a recent meeting of the American Association of School Librarians, one of the vendors who was selling online services to school districts and school libraries handed me promotional information in which he *bragged* about restricted access to the Internet. I find that a great many librarians are buying into the idea that the only way that they can get access to the Internet is if they do, indeed, "protect the children," whatever that means. Everyone seems to think that any time kids get on the Internet, they're going to go immediately to alt.sex.bestiality, and I really would like to know more about how in the library community we put some teeth into our ethical support of the First Amendment, instead of just caving into school districts that are running scared from the religious right and everybody else.

Godwin: I think there's a useful approach in Senator Patrick Leahy's alternative bill in which he says that rather than pass the Exon amendment which in effect turns every mention of sex on the Net into an obscene phone call, what we really need to do is study the problem and actually promote technologies that allow people to screen out material that they don't want to see at the individual level. Certainly in the interim, we are going to see providers saying they will deliver connectivity but will not carry the alt hierarchy of news groups and therefore children are safer. Of course the problem is that sex can get mentioned in the astronomy news groups and then what do you do? Keep in mind the idea that John Gilmore once articulated: The Internet interprets attempts at censorship as damage and routes around them. Attempts by people at the top level or at the intermediate levels to prevent us from seeing stuff, turn out not to work overall, and so really, the only philosophically acceptable strategy is also the only practical strategy, which is empowering users to make their own choices. And this includes empowering parents to make choices for their children.

Littman: It's important to teach our children to act responsibly in an online environment. We recently read about youngsters who downloaded information on how to make a bomb. How can we deal with these kinds of activities? As indicated, one way is through education in our schools. Another complementary approach is to hold school-sponsored training and instructional sessions for parents and guardians. Regardless of what we do, if a youngster has access to a computer at home, he or she can access any of these bulletin boards and download this type of data.

Godwin: Just to answer the question more concretely: Write your senators to please support Senator Leahy's bill. That will make a difference.

Jana Varlejs, Rutgers SCILS: Marlyn, you were talking about the double key kind of encryption. Would it be possible for a parent to have some sort of key that prevented access for their children, one that closed off certain things or that opened only certain things? Is that technically feasible?

Littman: I imagine that this is technically feasible. I talked about firewalls and how these types of devices can restrict access to information. So, here is another example of a way in which this technology can be used to limit data accessibility.

Sam Latini: In the wake of the Oklahoma bombing, watching CNN, I was chilled to hear some Senators and experts saying Americans might have to lose some rights in the future. Thinking of this in terms of the Internet, it raises the prospect that speech on the Internet which is offensive in some way will be clamped down, that there will be more regulation.

Littman: The clipper chip is an example of what the government can do intrusively in terms of monitoring information. What types of restriction are we going to allow? How much access will we permit? Access, as we have seen, can also be dangerous. There is no single approach to dealing with accessibility to material on the Internet. I think we are going to see a multiplicity of approaches. Even in school systems, which I have been surveying, there are any number of methods that are used. For instance, some schools are very restrictive in terms of Internet access. In certain cases, a teacher actually stands over a youngster to monitor computer activity and determines what the youngster will see online. Other schools take a different view. Their goal is to teach children how to make intelligent choices and be responsible online citizens.

Godwin: Here is the real fix for people who care about freedom of speech and are worrying about the government's willingness to crack down (governments, even the best ones, are always willing to crack down—it's just the nature of governments). If you want to try and immunize our society against that kind of crackdown with regard to information on the Net, what you do is build a consensus that censoring the Net is the wrong approach. We already have that consensus with libraries. For the most part, nowadays people don't try to censor libraries. We hear about every case that happens just because it is comparatively rare now. It would seem crazy to say to a municipal library, get rid of your chemistry books because it is possible to research how to build a bomb using those chemistry books. We also don't have prior restraint for almost all sorts of dangerous materials that are available in books. What we have to do is tell our policy makers again and again that we believe the same rights that we have when it comes to traditional media apply to this electronic medium as well.

One way we do it, by the way, is by participating in the medium ourselves. We have to be online, we have to teach other people to be online, we have to teach people to use the medium responsibly. We also have to talk these issues out so that people are ready to respond to the arguments that our policy makers, who are typically a generation or two behind us, are going to make when they're all too ready to regulate.

Elyse Robinson, Merck: I'm a patent searcher and so I'm interested in a couple of things that have to do with intellectual property and also have to do with availability of information. On the Internet, all of the 1994 patents are now available in full text. I have been looking into what is available from the N.I.H. (National Institutes of Health), which has its World Wide Web site, and from the National Library of Medicine, and the Geological Survey. In contrast to the U.S. Patent and Trademark Office, these other organizations basically have information for sale and I'm wondering what kind of copyright, what kind of information accessibility issues are out there?

Lape: Your comments are interesting to me for a couple of different reasons. One, the current administration's Working Group on Intellectual Property that I referred to earlier, has made a number of recommendations for changes, amendments to the Copyright Act. Their primary interest in the interrelationship between patent law and the Internet is the increase in availability of information about other inventions that is now already developing and will develop even more. This is of great interest to the Patent Office because this information about prior inventions, as you know, will be very important for determining what is prior art. As a result, this will make the job of the Patent Office to reject patent applications easier. That's basically what they're interested in at this point.

What appeared to me to be the second part of your comments about the copyright protection available for various databases, all of the information, that is, the facts and or ideas that are contained in any database, are clearly not protected by copyright and clearly can be copied by anybody. The problem is that information is always embedded in some kind of expression. I shouldn't say always, because there is this Supreme Court case, Feist, in which the white pages of a phone book were found to be just pure information with no expression, but it is very difficult to find data that isn't embedded in some expression. Therefore, the copyright protection for the form of expression ends up limiting access to the facts or the ideas that are embedded in the expression, because whoever put the data into whatever form it is in, and it is the form that is protected by copyright, can control distribution, i.e., copying of that data. Have I answered your question?

Robinson: One of the points of my question that I don't know that you have addressed was with regard to government information such as N.I.H. or N.T.I.S. information. I have found things coming out of the National Library of Medicine and the N.I.H. that are being made available for sale. I think you could even order them on the Internet but you couldn't actually get to the data itself, and it was my objective to get the data. If the objective is making information available, why aren't they putting it on the Internet? Is there some kind of copyright question—what is the question here?

Lape: It is a copyright question. Under current Section 105 of the Copyright Act, works of the federal government, that is, any work which is produced by an employee of the federal government within the scope of his or her employment, that is, anything that anybody who is an employee of the federal government writes or produces at work, is not subject to copyright protection. This would include presidential papers (watch that, next time some president wants to get a tax write-off for donating to a library papers in which he has no rights). The theoretical justification for Section 105 is two-fold. One, these are works that we have already paid for. Why should the public pay twice? Second, we want the works of the U.S. government—such as legislative history, statutes, cases—we want them all to be very freely available. We have a strong public interest in seeing that that material is widely and freely available. So, the basis upon which the N.I.H. is offering government information for sale eludes me.

Question: On the basis of distributional costs?

Lape: It may be the distributional cost, but then once a government work has been distributed the first time, you should be able to copy it because it is not protected by copyright. In other words, if you get hold of one copy of it, you ought to be able to just copy it again. That is, the government cannot prevent you from making an additional copy. But to get it initially out of them, that may be what they're using as leverage to exact that payment.

Godwin: I think there's a really interesting case now, it's not actually a case, but it will be, involving Westlaw. It is related to the fact that federal court decisions, under the Copyright Act's Section 105, are not copyrightable. However, West asserts a claim of copyright, and West as publisher is often the official reporter in many jurisdictions, maybe most. They claim a copyright based on their grammatical corrections, their page numbers and their key numbering system. I think their position is totally wrong. They take the position that even a minimal amount of added value is enough to make the information copyrightable. I think that position is wrong. I think that after the Feist case, what you really have is sort of a disguised sweat-of-the-brow argument that West is asserting and they are trying to disguise it and make it a creativity argument. It is just not very convincing. I think that ultimately this issue is going to be revisited by the Supreme Court and West is going to lose.

West's secret up to now has been this: They settle out of court. In other words, they make you litigate it up to a certain point and then they buy you off. They are paying their way into keeping the case from reaching the court. It is going to take a public interest group like Jamie Love's Taxpayer Assets Project to take this all the way in the court system, but it's going to happen at some point.

Jane Anne Hannigan, professor emerita, Columbia: This is a question on copyright, too. There's an increase in the establishment of home pages on the Internet; everybody seems to be creating them. You can insert graphics, photographs, text from all over, or your own text. Who owns the copyright when you then create the new product which is the home page?

Lape: When you take preexisting work such as graphics or text that you have obtained someplace else and then use it to create a new work, you're creating a derivative work. The new work is a work in which you can have copyright protection, so long as you were not infringing by borrowing the earlier work. If you infringe in borrowing the earlier work, then in most cases the new work won't have copyright protection. Your new copyright, that is the copyright you would have in the home page you have put together that has all of the other material in it, that copyright is in the selection, the choices that you made of what to include, what to exclude, where to put it, and so on. In other words, you don't thereby acquire copyright in the preexisting material, but you do have copyright protection in all of the creative choices that you made in assembling that material and arranging it and selecting and so on.

Question: Would including very small excerpts from other work be considered "fair use"?

Lape: Maybe; a big, big maybe. The courts, with the notable exception of the Acuff-Rose case recently, have been very, very reluctant to find much of anything to be fair use. They have been very, very protective, finding borrowing of tiny amounts to not be fair use. You certainly cannot use sheer volume as any kind of protection against a possible claim of copyright infringement. That said, people go about the business constantly of copying protected works, and hoping that what they are doing is in fact going to be fair use. But there is absolutely no yardstick, and I've heard people suggest yardsticks—a certain number of sentences per page, or a certain number of words—there is no yardstick.

Godwin: Let me offer another part of the answer. There's a peculiar problem associated with home pages, a very new problem, which concerns the link. The link is not a copy, therefore, link is not an infringement. What happens when you link to a copyrighted work and then people use your home page as a bridge to a copyrighted work, I don't know.

Lape: It might well turn out to be found to be contributory infringement. The question will be, is it contributory or not, and I have a feeling that the decision will turn on the extent to which you have been found to profit from doing this.

Schement: I have a question from the other side. Recently, several colleagues wrote and told me how much they enjoyed articles I had written that they had downloaded from the Internet, from what home pages, I have no idea. In fact, I didn't know the articles were on the Internet. All of them had been published in academic journals and so I guess my question is, what's happening to me there?

Comment: You are reaching a much broader audience!

Lape: Most academics don't complain about that kind of thing. First of all, it's going to depend on who owns the copyright in those articles. Frequently academic journals require assignment of copyright to the journal as a condition of publication. The first question is who owns the copyright? Secondly, is anyone interested in suing for the infringement which apparently occurred as a result of someone scanning your articles in. You would only want to pursue such a course of action if there really were some sense in it.

Schement: I'll tell you what I'm really interested in. One of my fears is that what is being downloaded is not what I wrote, but my name is associated with it.

Lape: That was the comment that I was going to make next. A risk that academics who normally want the widest possible dissemination of their works take is that other people will edit what you have written and then send it on with your name associated with it. We have no kind of moral rights protection in this country that would protect that interest, the interest that you have in not having your name associated with something that isn't in a form in which you actually wrote it. Our moral rights legislation doesn't protect an article, for example, that you might write. But, of course, there would be possibly other kinds of causes of action: An unfair competition claim, for instance, under section 43 (a) of the Lanham Act would be very likely to succeed. You can bring an unfair competition claim if someone is passing off something that you produced as his or something that he produced as yours.

Godwin: Also, in the tort arena you have a couple of invasion of privacy torts, including misappropriation of name and a false likeness representation.

Schement: For those of you who have an historical interest, you probably already have thought that the current situation is not so different from the situation that existed in the first fifty to one hundred years of the invention of printing, when all sorts of materials were being printed regardless of the proper citation or accuracy or anything else. People were just getting into print and whoever had the press was printing and distributing material as rapidly as possible. From an historical interest, of course, today that's fascinating, but I can imagine that at the time, it wasn't so fascinating.

Chelton: The thought has occurred to me, in listening to the two lawyers here, that years ago when I took a course in ethics, there was something about the essence of a law being that it was enforceable. The more I listen to the two of you, the more I worry that neither the First Amendment nor copyright is enforceable in this electronic environment, even given the historical perspective. I worry whether there is something at greater risk here than whether these laws can be enforced in the way they were intended—are we looking at a lawless kind of void on the frontier?

Lape: Your comment brings to mind an article recently published in the *Cardozo Arts & Entertainment Law Journal* by Jessica Litman, entitled, "The Exclusive Right to Read." She argues very persuasively that our Copyright Act is way too long, way too complex, contains too many counter-intuitive provisions that nobody who is not a copyright lawyer can make head nor tail of, and that it is unenforceable because nobody knows what it says, nobody abides by it anyway, and that what we need to do is scrap the whole thing. She suggests a copyright act that is no longer than three pages and can be understood by an elementary school student. The Working Group on Intellectual Property has also suggested that we need to educate the public. Now, their concern about educating the public seems to be largely a matter of persuading the public that just about anything that you do is going to be copyright infringement and you better not try and do any of it.

Godwin: I have a different answer for copyright and a different answer for the First Amendment. One of the things that we're now facing is that the drafters of the Copyright Act never anticipated a day when everybody would be a potential infringer. Fifty years ago, if I wrote a book and you wanted to be an infringer, you had to have your own printing presses and distribution system. It was easy to find you, easy to sue you most of the time, unless you were in a foreign country, and even then it was usually pretty easy to track you down. Policing copyright interests was relatively easy and it made a lot of sense to "incentivize" writers (forgive that neologism), because copying was a sufficiently difficult and capital intensive thing to do. It was a very good locus for remunerating writers and scientists. But now we live in a world in which it is trivially easy to "publish." You can put a whole novel on a floppy disk. You could put more than one, and distribute it to a thousand of your closest friends in the blink of an eye through a listserv, or a hundred thousand if you post it through a news group. The problem is that although, theoretically, this kind of distribution is just as policeable as the old kind, as a practical matter it may not be.

So I think that there is some chance that new balances will be struck in the adaptation of copyright law. I'm not sure this means the death of copyright law. Some people have predicted that. But it certainly means that new balances will be struck just as they have been struck with regard to things like home taping and use of photo copiers. The First Amendment is different in this sense. The First Amendment is enforced every time you speak freely, so if you want to enforce it, speak freely.

Varlejs: You mentioned that you disagreed with the American Library Association's guideline on intellectual property. Could you elaborate a little bit on that? Could you tell us what you think might be a better guideline?

Lape: This is the statement on fair use in the electronic age, dated January 18, 1995 (see Appendix A). There are two aspects of the statement that I criticize. One, in the introductory material, the statement characterizes the balance as being a balance between copyright owners' interest in getting money for their works and the public's interest in access.

That is not the classic balance of policies. The classic balance of copyright policies is the public's need for there to be enough incentive to create so that people will create works and the public's need for access. In other words, the public's need is really on both sides of the balance. So, I was simply criticizing the characterization of the policies behind copyright law. I think it is important to keep in mind what the policies really are because otherwise you start talking about the interests of copyright owners in making money, as if we had a public policy in serving that interest—and we don't. We simply don't.

The other aspect of the statement which I criticize concerns the question of whether a recipient of a transmission over a network is liable or not. That is, whether you are liable for turning on your computer and pressing enough keys so that something appears on your screen or something is downloaded into your computer, whether doing that would be a basis for imposing liability on the recipient of transmissions. This is a concern which has been raised by a number of people and it appears from the ALA statement that the ALA is suggesting that this be dealt with as a matter of fair use, in other words, that we try and argue that it is fair use to receive the transmissions. That is not going to be a good way to protect the power of ordinary people to receive transmissions on their computers for the following reasons: Fair use is always an ad hoc determination; it is decided on a case by case basis. There aren't any generalized rules. You do not want to have to argue on a case by case basis for fair use every time somebody downloads something into his computer. Secondly, fair use determinations are based largely on the public utility of the particular use at issue. So, you would have to argue how much public utility is there in having this person read this particular thing. That is not the theoretical basis that I would use to argue that recipients of transmissions aren't liable.

Anne Ciliberti, William Paterson University: What would be your argument?

Lape: The argument is that by analogy, recipients of other kinds of infringing works have never been held liable under our law. If you go into a bookstore and you buy an infringing book, you are not liable. If you go into a movie theater and you watch an infringing movie, you are not going to be held liable. By analogy, the same sorts of rules are to apply in the network environment as well.

Schement: What if I buy a pirated video tape?

Lape: Same thing. With very, very few exceptions, purchasers of infringing material have not been held liable. The argument could be made that they should be held liable as contributory infringers because they create the market which encourages the distributor to distribute the infringing material. But they have not been held liable. The only case I've seen on point, that is, where liability was found on the part of a purchaser, was *Demetriades v. Kaufmann,* a 1988 decision in the Southern District of New York in which a couple had asked an architect to build them a house that looked just like the so-and-so's house. They were included among the defendants that got sued for copyright infringement. They admitted copyright liability — why they did that, I don't know. They were held liable by the court.

Dave Wilson, Rutgers Master's in Communication and Information Studies (MCIS) student: The other day I was reading something about cyberspace that talked about how marketers could develop profiles about me based on things that I've put up as postings on the Internet. My question is, if I copyright my postings, am I protecting myself in any way from them compiling these profiles of me?

Lape: You don't have to do anything to have copyright protection in what you produce other than fix it in some tangible medium of expression. So, you don't need to register a copyright, for example, in order for the expression to be protected. You have protection in what you produce, assuming it has sufficient originality, which it probably does. Now, there are a number of issues raised by your question: How are they getting access to the postings? Are they copying sufficient amounts of material from your posting in order to infringe? If all they're doing is looking at your posting and seeing that you're interested in dogs, just as an example, that would not be copyright infringement. Lifting information and using it is not going to ever be copyright infringement.

Cindy Jablonowski, MCIS student: I publish intellectual information for a technical society. We publish proceedings which contain edited governmental works. In order to provide access to that material, we have to publish at a profit. Right now we're grappling with putting things online, standards, and such, and on the Internet, and we are concerned about losing the profitability. If we lose the profit, the audience will in turn lose the access because we won't be able to compile these works and produce them. So, I think there's a closer relationship between the profit and the access than you seem to feel there is. I mean, if we can't afford to sell these profitably, we can't compile the information and we can't produce it in a form that is accessible to the public.

Lape: I think your point is well taken. You really are talking about the rationale behind copyright protection. The reason for offering the incentive is to get the works produced. Why do we offer the incentive? It is so that producers like yourself will then have the funds and the motivation to put together the works. We want the works disseminated. Why is it that we want the works disseminated? Because we want the information that's in them to be freely available to people. So, I think that your point is well taken. Your works are protected by copyright as soon as you produce them. You want to make sure, though, to put on the works an appropriate copyright notice. You also want to specify clearly if there are any uses that you want people to be able to make of the works. In other words, if you are willing to license certain further uses of the materials that you're distributing, that should appear in the materials. You want to make sure to register them with the Copyright Office. The registration is fairly inexpensive and will preserve the possibility of getting statutory damages and attorney's fees. These are special rights that are provided for by the Act and unless you have registered within three months of publication, you stand to lose those rights. So you want to register within three months of the first publication.

Varlejs: Some months ago in one of the libraries in New Jersey that provides Internet connections for its users, one of the users somehow broke into Cornell's computer and did some damage. Cornell then said to the New Jersey library that provided the open access that the library was liable. What do you think of that?

Littman: I mentioned that I had spoken with Alan Liddle who is a lieutenant commander in the Royal Navy and Professor of Information Systems at the National Defense University. Lieutenant Commander Liddle said that if your library is used as a jumping-off point by infiltrators to invade other networks, then your library is responsible for damages incurred. In fact, some cases are currently under investigation. I will defer to the attorneys now.

Godwin: I get asked this question all the time and it's going to be a factual determination. It depends on how lousy your security is and how responsible you are for its lousiness. Basically, this is a standard negligence kind of analysis and if you were non-negligent and someone still managed to get in, you are not going to be held liable. You may have to prove it. At this point I would say, in general, the hazard is not yet so great that you're going to find it easy to get insurance coverage because many insurers do not even really recognize that as a risk. In the long run, maybe the type of site you are may put you in a risk class. For example, if you are a university site where you typically have a lot of intellectually creative individuals coming in every year exploring the nooks and crannies of your system, you may have more risk associated in that environment than you might have in a military computer where they have other sanctions for people who misbehave.

Littman: I think this is an emerging area of concern and underscores the need to take seriously security mechanisms that are selected and implemented on your network.

Robinson: This also has to do with the security issue. On the one hand you were saying that it's really hard to prosecute people who are putting information on the Net. It's hard to have copyright protection over material being redistributed on the Net. On the other hand, you're talking about the lack of security—people being able to tap into your interactions on the Net, people being able to watch what you're doing. I'm kind of lost at the dichotomy of this. So I want to ask a specific question and then for your more general comments. When I am using Netscape or World Wide Web or even gophers, how susceptible am I to viruses? I believe I'm outside the firewall in what I believe is a network node, although it's possible I'm inside the firewall?

Godwin: I'll just tell you, you're not susceptible to any significant degree from using Netscape.

Littman: But what happens if the individual downloads a file?

Godwin: Netscape is a browser. It's not going to infect you. What will infect you? Downloading stuff that is infected can infect you. So if you use Netscape to move a file over to your system that happens to be infected in some way, that could infect it. But, using Netscape by itself, inside or outside a firewall (I'm not even sure how to sensibly talk about that when you're talking about Netscape), the mere use of the browser is not going to infect you. Typically, downloading files is not going to infect you. Typically, you've got to download an application. As Marlyn said, normally you have to have a host for a virus. But what I always tell people to do is when they have a work station and you have a mouse for your work station, put a condom over the mouse. I find that that tends to make people feel secure and who am I to tell them any different.

Littman: I can't top that one.

Appendix A:
Fair Use in the Electronic Age:
Serving the Public Interest

American Library Association

Whereas, The statement, "Fair Use in the Electronic Age: Serving the Public Interest," is an outgrowth of discussions among a number of library associations regarding intellectual property, and in particular, the concern that the interests and rights of copyright owners and users remain balanced in the digital environment; and

Whereas, The purpose of the statement is to outline the lawful uses of copyrighted works by individuals, libraries, and educational institutions in the electronic environment; and

Whereas, The statement is intended to inform ongoing copyright discussions and serve as a reference document for users and libraries, to be circulated widely, to spark discussion on these issues, and to provide feedback to the library associations; and

Whereas, The statement will, for these reasons, continue to be a work in progress; now, therefore, be it

Resolved, That the American Library Association supports in principle the working document, "Fair Use in the Electronic Age: Serving the Public Interest."

Adopted by the Council of the American
Library Association
February 8, 1995

Elizabeth Martinez
Secretary of the Council

Working Document   1/18/95

Fair Use in the Electronic Age:
Serving the Public Interest

The primary objective of copyright is not to reward the labor of authors, but "[t]o promote the Progress of Science and useful Arts." To this end, copy-

ALA Council Document 20.10, approved in principle, February 8, 1995.

right assures authors the right to their original expression, but encourages others to build freely upon the ideas and information conveyed by a work.... This result is neither unfair nor unfortunate. It is the means by which copyright advances the progress of science and art.

> Justice Sandra Day O'Connor
> Feist Publications, Inc. v. Rural Telephone
> Service Co., 499 US 340, 349 (1991)

The genius of United States copyright law is that, in conformance with its constitutional foundation, it balances the intellectual property interests of authors, publishers and copyright owners with society's need for the free exchange of ideas. Taken together, fair use and other public rights to utilize copyrighted works, as confirmed in the Copyright Act of 1976, constitute indispensable legal doctrines for promoting the dissemination of knowledge, while ensuring authors, publishers and copyright owners appropriate protection of their creative works and economic investments.

The fair use provision of the Copyright Act allows reproduction and other uses of copyrighted works under certain conditions for purposes such as criticism, comment, news reporting, teaching (including multiple copies for classroom use), scholarship or research. Additional provisions of the law allow uses specifically permitted by Congress to further educational and library activities. The preservation and continuation of these balanced rights in an electronic environment as well as in traditional formats are essential to the free flow of information and to the development of an information infrastructure that serves the public interest.

It follows that the benefits of the new technologies should flow to the public as well as to copyright proprietors. As more information becomes available only in electronic formats, the public's legitimate right to use copyrighted material must be protected. In order for copyright to truly serve its purpose of "promoting progress," the public's right of fair use must continue in the electronic era, and these lawful uses of copyrighted works must be allowed without individual transaction fees.

Without infringing copyright, the public has a right to expect:

- to read, listen to, or view publicly marketed copyrighted material privately, on site or remotely;
- to browse through publicly marketed copyrighted material;
- to experiment with variations of copyrighted material for fair use purposes, while preserving the integrity of the original;
- to make or have made for them a first generation copy for personal use of an article or other small part of a publicly marketed copyrighted work or a work in a library's collection for such purpose as study, scholarship, or research; and
- to make transitory copies if ephemeral or incidental to a lawful use and if retained only temporarily.

Without infringing copyright, nonprofit libraries and other Section 108 libraries, on behalf of their clientele, should be able:

- to use electronic technologies to preserve copyrighted materials in their collections;
- to provide copyrighted materials as part of electronic reserve room service;
- to provide copyrighted materials as part of electronic interlibrary loan service; and
- to avoid liability, after posting appropriate copyright notices, for the unsupervised actions of their users.

Users, libraries, and educational institutions have a right to expect:

- that the terms of licenses will not restrict fair use or other lawful library or educational uses;
- that U.S. government works and other public domain materials will be readily available without restrictions and at a government price not exceeding the marginal cost of dissemination; and
- that rights of use for nonprofit education apply in face-to-face teaching and in transmittal or broadcast to remote locations where educational institutions of the future must increasingly reach their students.

Carefully constructed copyright guidelines and practices have emerged for the print environment to ensure that there is a balance between the rights of users and those of authors, publishers, and copyright owners. New understandings, developed by all stakeholders, will help to ensure that this balance is retained in a rapidly changing electronic environment. This working statement addresses lawful uses of copyrighted works in both the print and electronic environments.

January 18, 1995

This statement was developed by representatives of the following associations:

American Association of Law Libraries
American Library Association
Association of Academic Health Sciences
   Library Directors

Association of Research Libraries
Medical Library Association
Special Libraries Association

Appendix B:
Excerpts from Principles for the Development of the National Information Infrastructure,

including "NREN and the National Infrastructure: Policy Decisions for Libraries" by Fred W. Weingarten

American Library Association

Proceedings: Principles for the Development of the National Information Infrastructure[1]

September 8–10, 1993, Washington, D.C.

Supported by ALA, LITA, CLR with assistance from the National Science Foundation and from the participating organizations

Executive Summary

Representatives from fifteen national library and information associations met September 8th through 10th in Washington, DC to discuss critical national policy issues dealing with the National Information Infrastructure (NII), sometimes called the National Data Highway.

The group reached a consensus on key principles and questions that must be used to guide the development of plans for the evolution of the NII in the areas of:

- First Amendment
- Privacy
- Intellectual Property
- Ubiquity
- Equitable Access
- Interoperability

[1]*Reprinted with permission; full text available from ALA LITA.*

There was strong agreement among the diverse group that libraries will play several key roles in the evolution of the national infrastructure,
- As both providers and consumers of information,
- As public access points to the information infrastructure,
- As responsible for protecting the public interest in access to information.

testing of plans, legislation and approaches to the major issues involved with the ambitious national information infrastructure undertaking.

The organizations participating were:

AALL	American Association of Law Libraries
AASL	American Association of School Librarians
ACRL	Association of College and Research Libraries
ALA	American Library Association
ALA	Committee on Legislation
ALA	Ad Hoc Subcommittee on Telecommunications
ALA	Committee on Intellectual Freedom
ALISE	Association for Library & Information Science Education
ARL	Association of Research Libraries
ASCLA	Association of Specialized and Cooperative Library Agencies
ASIS	American Society for Information Science
CLR	Council on Library Resources
COSLA	Chief Officers of State Library Agencies
CNI	Coalition for Networked Information
LITA	Library and Information Technology Association
MLA	Medical Library Association
PLA	Public Library Association
SLA	Special Libraries Association

1. Introduction and Background

The goal of the forum was to provide a mechanism for the library community to identify national policy issues, questions and principles in the areas of telecommunications and information infrastructure. The structured policy issues forum brought together representatives of the American Library Association (ALA) and several other library and related associations, with special attention to representation from all sizes and types of libraries. A set of principles was developed to identify commonalities, to inform and guide association activities and to enable individual librarians and libraries to make decisions in an informed context.

This is a critical time as many groups are developing conflicting visions of the National Information Infrastructure (NII), whom it will serve, and how it will be developed. This is also a critical time in the redefinition of libraries as the diffusion of the new information technology reshapes the services and the demands on libraries. Their role as institutions has been one of enabling access to information, not just providing access to books. Libraries are both clients and servers in the infrastructure.

The forum focused on policy issues dealing with NII, using the experienced representatives to relate efforts in the general information policy area to the new areas identified with the NII. The questions were derived as an approach to test strategies and plans that have been or will be developed, for instance, by a number of groups:

- Congress
- The Administration
- Regulatory agencies
- Educational associations
- State and local governments
- Industry groups
- Other constituencies.

This document is the product of the forum and the review and editing by the planning committee and editor. It is meant to be a starting point and is not meant to be seen as a finished and endorsed document. It is a working draft in a continuing process.

2. Approach

Dr. Michael Nelson, senior policy analyst for the Office of Science and Technology Policy, opened the conference with a talk about the National Information Infrastructure issues and the Administration's plans and approach. The key points in his talk were:

- The Administration plans to spend money to get technology to people. It plans to use the Commerce Department to provide matching programs to allow access through supporting the introduction of computers in schools. The program, which will be built on a previous program, should grow to over $150 million per year. This can be called the "off ramps" to the national data highway.
- Currently telecommunications policy is made in many different arenas. The policies have evolved through the interaction of differing regulatory approaches that included the courts, the FCC, the PUC. However, these policies evolved in the fifties, and do not match the new technology.
- This Administration intends to take a proactive approach to the development of a coherent policy, rather than just let the lobbyists fight it out. A key element in the development of new policies is the new National Information Infrastructure Task Force that will be chaired by Secretary of Commerce, Ron Brown.
- Some of the issues that need to be addressed are:
  - Privacy and security
  - Intellectual property rights
  - Fair use
  - Applications of the NII
  - Regulations: timeliness of the current ones and the need for new ones
  - How to identify public interest and goals in the evolution of the NII
- There are four strands in the information infrastructure: hardware, services, applications and the people served. The Government is most interested in the services and needs to act as a stimulus for the private development of the hardware and applications.

Dr. Weingarten, who is executive director of the Computing Research Association, discussed his paper (Appendix E) and presented a brief introduction to the issues of policy making where:

- There are at least three ways of approaching the development of public policy:
  1) The expert view. Experts could be identified to define the problems and then solve them. In theory, but seldom in practice, the results will be so impressive that all parties would agree.
  2) The bureaucratic approach (public administration). The affected agencies review the issues in the context of their budgets, their constituencies and their charters.
  3) The political processes. The situation is seen as a process of conflict, where various elements take positions in a high stakes arena. The winners and losers fight over the stakes, and their use weapons—which may be Congress or the courts—to shape the battle.
- The stakes in this debate are high. The business information market is huge:

Areas (from a 1990 Harvard study)	Billions
Telecom and computing	$272
Broadcasting and Entertainment	$88
Publishing and print	$145
Information services	$359
Total	$864+

- There are three dimensions of conflict over the NII:
  1) Social and economic goals and values
  2) National, local and international goals and values
  3) Various stakeholder goals and values.

- There is a debate over the process where different areas have different values that are shaped by their constraints. Some of these areas include the President's Science Advisor, the Economic Council, the FCC, Congress, etc. Also, there is a fight over stakeholder access, where the effort is spent to control or limit the agenda.
- We have reached this point through four major trends:
  1) Federal science networking
  2) Technology advances
  3) User networking
  4) Deregulation.

A key assumption is that regulatory approaches lag technology advances.

- Critical history for steps in the evolution of the network and then NII included:
  - Dartmouth basic and time-sharing
  - Regional computing centers, remote batch and then time sharing
  - ARPAnet and e-mail
  - BITNET and grass roots
  - The PC and campus networks
  - Internet and NSFNET
- There is a three-way tension in the evolution of the network between the research needs which require very high bandwidths (gigabits for individual applications); scholarship, education and public information needs that require gigabits but which can be aggregated; and everybody else's needs for high bandwidth with an emphasis on multimedia applications and use.
- The [Weingarten] paper discusses the technology trends of speed, integration of computers and communications, digital format that are all pushing these issues. The paper also addresses the key questions of:
  - What capabilities should it have?
  - What should it cost?
  - Who should pay?
  - Who should run it?
  - What are the rules?
  - Who can use it?
  - What is the government role?
- There are five layers of policy:
  - Process
  - Infrastructure building
  - Information policy
  - Applications and users
  - Societal impacts
- In summary, the debate is among the differing stakeholders and their perspectives, the framing of the processes and arenas, the major issues and how to strike bargains between the players.

Mr. Ken Kay, who is executive director of the Computer Systems Policy Project (CSPP), an affiliation of chief executive officers of American computer companies, presented comments from his personal perspective, from that of the computer industry (CSPP) and from the view of what libraries should do next. His remarks included:

- What is emerging is a profound change in how we communicate and what powers are available to the individual. One example is SeniorNet with over 10,000 individuals in San Francisco communicating and accessing information. Some of the information that now can be accessed includes databases which can help with developing preventative health care strategies. There will be a significant impact on the economy and business. There will be winners, but there will also be losers. We should note that the Howard Johnsons came after the highways were built, not before.
- The CSPP was formed in 1989 and provided advice about the High Performance Computing and Communication program. It supported the basic idea and recommended changes to broaden the vision to include a focus on individuals and the applications that benefited them such as health care, or education or manufacturing. Two major efforts are underway now:
  1) To develop a consensus by the research community on an agenda for the necessary research projects to support the evolution of the NII;
  2) To publish a report in December which suggests rather than "solving the telecommunications problem" that we focus on interoperability so as to avoid the Balkanization of the services.

- The library community has played an important role in the NII evolution and debate. There is a need for the vision of stakeholders other than from industry. The libraries will play a key role in the access to applications. Librarians need to tell their story well in order to reshape their role perceived by many now that will limit the scope of their potential contributions.

3. Principles

The major principles identified during the forum discussion were:
- First Amendment
- Privacy
- Intellectual Property
- Ubiquity
- Equitable Access
- Interoperability

Principles for the Development of the National Information Infrastructure

FIRST AMENDMENT/INTELLECTUAL FREEDOM

1. Access to the NII should be available and affordable to all regardless of age, religion, disability, sexual orientation, social and political views, national origin, economic status, location, information literacy, etc.
2. The NII service providers must guarantee the free flow of information protected by the First Amendment.
3. The NII should support and encourage a diversity of information providers.
4. Individuals should have the right to choose what information to receive through the NII.

PRIVACY

1. Privacy should be carefully protected and extended.
2. Comprehensive policies should be developed to ensure that the privacy of all people is protected.
3. Personal data collected to provide specific services should be limited to the minimum necessary.
4. Sharing data collected from individuals should only be permitted with their informed consent.
5. Individuals should have the right to inspect and correct data files about themselves.
6. Transaction data should remain confidential.

INTELLECTUAL PROPERTY

1. Intellectual property rights and protections are independent of the form of publication or distribution.
2. The intellectual property system should ensure a fair and equitable balance between rights of creators and other copyright owners and the needs of users.
3. Fair use and other exceptions to owners' rights in the copyright law should continue in the electronic environment.
4. Compensation systems must provide a fair and reasonable return to copyright owners.

UBIQUITY

1. Libraries should preserve and enhance their traditional roles in providing public access to information regardless of format.
2. Network access costs for libraries, educational organizations, government entities and non-profit groups should be stable, predictable and location insensitive.
3. Resources must be allocated to provide basic public access in fostering the development of the information infrastructure.

EQUITABLE ACCESS

1. The NII should support and encourage a diversity of information providers in order to guarantee an open, fair, and competitive marketplace, with a full range of viewpoints.
2. Diversity of access should be protected through use of non-proprietary protocols.
3. Access to basic network services should be affordable and available to all.
4. Basic network access should be made available independent of geographic location.
5. The NII should ensure private, government and non-profit participation in governance of the network.
6. Electronic information should be appropriately documented, organized and archived through the cooperative endeavors of information service providers and libraries.

INTEROPERABILITY

1. The design of the NII should facilitate two-way, audio, video and data communication from anyone to anyone easily and effectively.
2. Interoperability standards should be encouraged and tied to incentives for the use of those standards in awards for Federal funding.
3. A transition phase should provide compatibility between leading edge technology and trailing edge technology to allow users reasonable protection from precipitate change.
4. The Federal government should encourage interoperability standards and should tie incentives to the use of those standards.
5. Federal government information dissemination programs should adhere to interoperability standards.
6. Principles of interoperability should require directory and locator services and non-proprietary search protocols as well as a minimal set of data elements for the description of data bases.

NREN and the National Infrastructure: Policy Decisions for Libraries

Fred C. Weingarten
Executive Director, Computer Research Association

Introduction

In less than a decade, the Internet has become a worldwide resource—an indispensable tool for the research and education community. Now, spurred by the success of the Internet, a new political vision—creating a new National Information Infrastructure (NII)—has begun to dominate the communications policy debate. The NII was a major element of the Clinton/Gore campaign platform, and the new administration is actively promoting the vision. It was a core element, although developed in only very general terms, of the administration's Technology Plan released in February of this year, and a White House Interagency Task Force is busily working to put flesh on the concept. Congress is considering several bills directed at creating an NII.

The computer and information industries, the telecommunication industry, and many public interest groups have all endorsed the need for such a national program, although their views of what the NII should look like diverge widely.

It seems clear that technological, political, and economic forces are combining to energize the creation of the NII, and that it will materialize in some form or other. Over the next few years, basic decisions in government and in the private sector will be made that will determine the fundamental characteristics of the NII. Users, particularly organizations such as libraries that are intensive users of information, need to formulate their own visions and participate actively in shaping the NII.

To do so will be a difficult endeavor. Although a few public interest and consumer groups have long been active in communications policy, this is in general an uncharacteristic role for most users. Furthermore, it has not been common to take user needs into consideration in making communication policy, again beyond a certain broad, common denominator level of concern over rates.

Technical Characteristics of the NII

Both the capability and the demand for a new NII are the product of technological change in both computers and communications. Advances in microelectronics and fiber optics have been major drivers, of course. But, so also have been other technical advances in areas such as software engineering, data structures, visualization, and computer architecture served to open up new possibilities, particularly for applications. Whatever their differences among themselves over details of their visions, most stakeholders agree that an NII would have the following technological characteristics:

- Speed. NII transmission speeds will be substantially faster than the current telephone network, although it is not yet clear how fast it will be hundreds of thousands, millions, or billions of bits per second. Technological capabilities are improving rapidly, as are the demands for speed.
- Integration of Computer and Communications. Computer and communication technologies are being woven together inextricably. Distributed computing applications are placing increasing demands on the capacity of the communications system, and computing is being imbedded in the network. In some cases, so tightly are they coupled that to computer scientists, when several computers are linked together with a very high speed network, that collection, itself, is beginning to resemble a single distributed, parallel computer.
- Digital Formats. Information in digital (as opposed to analog) format not only is transmitted more reliably and quickly, but it is in a form directly usable by computers. That means that, not only can the information be stored, manipulated, and displayed in many ways, it can be recognized and interpreted within the transmission system, which is, itself, computer controlled.
- Portability. Although it will probably not replace wire or fiber as the dominant two-way communication link to the home or office, digital radio is already beginning to free users from depending on wires, and that trend will continue. AT&T is promising "personal phone numbers" with connectivity anywhere, any time. Some lap top computers already come equipped with cellular modems. Some computer manufacturers refer to "nomadic" computing as the future pattern.
- Multimedia. In digital encoding, all forms of information, sound, computer data, images, or text "look alike" to the system at some basic level, allowing them all to be handled in the same way and by the NII for storage, transmission, or processing.
- Multiple uses. The NII will carry a wide variety of applications and services, in contrast with the current telephone, broadcast or cable television systems, each of which was created to provide a very narrow range of services.
- Flexibility. Much of the capability of the new NII will reside in its computer software and data bases, rather than in the fixed hardware. Hence, the system will be far more flexible and able to support a wide variety of services, some of which may not even yet be imagined.

The Need for a User Perspective

Beneath this list of general technical characteristics, however, lies a host of difficult, still unanswered questions, many of them raised or complicated by the very flexibility that makes NII so attractive. For instance:

- Exactly what technical capabilities should the NII have? The list of capabilities above leaves much to be decided. Exactly how fast should the network be, particularly in the so-called "last mile," the lines that connect to the user in his or her home or office. How heterogeneous? On which transmission standards and network architecture should it be based? The answers to these questions will determine the range of services and resources that will be available over the NII.

- How much will (or should) the NII cost? A key trade-off with technical sophistication is cost. How much do we as a society want to invest in a new infrastructure? Some advocates are proposing a very low-cost ISDN system using most of the current copper infrastructure now in place. At the other extreme, estimates for an extremely high capacity system based on optical fiber to the home run as high as $400 billion.
- Who should pay for the NII? Who will ultimately pick up this bill? Barring the unlikely event that government finds extra money lying around, the private sector will make the investment. Traditionally with telephony, that investment has been passed along to all consumers in their telephone bill with some adjustments being made to keep the cost of basic service low. In the first place, everyone was considered to benefit from improvement in the service. Secondly, telephone service was the principal source of revenue for the phone companies; they had nowhere else to turn for income. The policy arguments came within that rather narrow framework of rates—that is, to what degree should long-distance rates be set higher and used to subsidize local rates. To what degree should rates for business users be set higher and subsidize basic level service for the home? (An important point here is that we have a precedent for differential pricing and using higher priced services to subsidize certain other services. This particular system of cross subsidizing could not be sustained for a variety of reasons in recent years, one of the major motivations for deregulation.)

What is the appropriate reasoning in this new NII? Will everyone find it equally beneficial? If the sale of information services provides the largest revenue stream, as many expect, should those service providers pay for the infrastructure? Should the physical carriers be allowed to offer higher level services as an incentive for them to invest in the network? This issue leads to the next cluster of questions.

- Who should run the NII and what spectrum of services should the physical network operators be allowed to offer? Some of the fiercest battles are now underway over this set of issues. Organizations are competing with one another for the rights to install and operate the infrastructure. Part of that fight is over the question of how broad a range of services they will be allowed to provide. Traditions in telephony and broadcast differ sharply on this point. Complicating the picture even more is the recent wave of mergers among previous competitors, telephone and cable, long distance and cellular telephony, information providers and distributors. These mergers, as well as decisions in the courts allowing or barring line-of-business restrictions, may remove some roadblocks and create larger pools of investment capital, but they may also preclude policy choices.
- Who should be able to use the NII? Access to the infrastructure is a many faceted issue. Many potential barriers to access exist, from physical limitations, to high cost, and the ability to use modern information technology. Some of these issues are analogous to questions that have arisen in the cases of telephony or broadcast; some are new. For instance, telephone conversations are inherently two-way, symmetric in terms of speaking and listening. In that case, access means the ability to participate, equally to speak and to listen. Broadcast and cable, on the other hand, have been asymmetric. The ability to view is not the same as the ability to transmit. In the world of cable, public access channels represent a limited attempt to provide some rights of the public to transmit. But that is a very limited right, and access is still very uneven in the mass media. (Interestingly, VCR has, in contrast, been a democratizing technology, lowering the entry cost and complexity of producing programs.)

The NII offers a new world of services. Some are still two-way communications;

some are still one-way massmedia services. Some, like bulletin boards, exhibit a completely different character. Defining what is meant by access will be a major and difficult issue of key importance to users. Traditional service providers may be inclined to apply their model to all services they provide.

- What should be the role of Federal and local governments? Of course, for many years, that question was answered simply. A private monopoly provides the service, government at both levels regulates—EVERYTHING. Over the last decade, we have steadily deregulated telecommunications. In part this was in recognition of the technological reality that monopolistic and rigid government control of the system at all points was not possible and to make the attempt would simply warp and inhibit the modernization of our infrastructure. Of course, deregulation also happened to be compatible with the acknowledged political and ideological tenor of the last two decades.

That is not to say that the issue has been resolved completely. State and local governments, as well as the courts, retain many controls over the communications system. Some of those residual controls may, indeed, constitute barriers to the evolution of the system. Clearly, government policy must be in response to public interest. If communications were, in the words of a past FCC chairman, the market equivalent to a toaster, there is no justification for much regulation other than consumer safety. Arguments for government intervention, then, must be accompanied by clear statements of the PUBLIC PURPOSE to be accomplished by that intervention.

All of these questions might be called "Infrastructure Policy" questions, since they concern the construction and operation of the basic NII communications system. "Information policy," on the other hand, is the term used for issues that concern the "stuff" of the infrastructure, the information and services that flow over the conduit. This distinction is becoming increasingly difficult to keep. Just as computers and communications technology are merging, so the concepts of conduit and content are becoming increasingly difficult to keep separate. This merging creates new difficulties for telecommunication policy makers, since they have traditionally treated those two domains as distinct.

Most particularly, that distinction has been used to keep users out of the communications policy debate (or, at least, bound their participation), by arguing that communications policy simply involves "technology" decisions. In the current communication system, particularly telephony, content is simply not a major domain of policy and the conduits are the switched telephone network. User interests rarely go beyond rates (to be low), ubiquity (to be universal), and quality (to be understandable).

The NII, on the other hand, is envisioned as combining several traditional services (telephony and cable television, for instance) and, additionally, supporting a vast array of new information services, many yet to be imagined. Although policies on broadcast, cable, or telephony could be narrowly focused on delivery of those specific services, the domain of policy on the NII will be exceptionally broad. The NII will support a wide variety of uses and communities of users. Technological choices, then, since they will strongly affect who can use the system and for what, cannot be made with the same detachment from information policy, and from users.

Some policy makers assert that infrastructure design is simply "technology" and, therefore, the proper domain of engineers and industry. They promise that "policy," referring to information policy, will come later. As can be seen above, this argument simply ignores the deep implications technological choices can have on critical public interests. Furthermore, it assures that powerful economic interests are sitting at the table before the public interest is admitted to the room.

Another important, perhaps pivotal point is that the definition of an infrastructure commonly includes the organizations, social structures, and services that are integral to its useful operation. In the past, that broader definition has been unimportant to telecommunications policy. The service, telephony, was inseparably linked to the wires and switches that were the medium, and the provider of the medium also provided the service. There is no other case of such large corporations dealing directly with their end-user customers, no matter how small, without intermediaries such as retail stores, agents, and the like. (This history may be distorting the communication companies' views of the information marketplace and their role in it. That market structure is likely to be far more diverse and multi-layered, as it is already in the case of the print industry.)

Libraries are organizational constituents, along with schools and research laboratories. As public information institutions, they, in some sense, need to participate in the policy debate both as users of the NII, but also as organizational parts of it, as providers of services.

Contrasting Views of the NII

Much of this confusion over policy seems to stem from different views of the nature of the National Research and Education Network (NREN) and its relationship with the NII. The NREN is variously seen as:

- A platform for research and development in ultra-high-speed communications systems and applications of them.
- A playground for a technological elite, for hackers and companion explorers of a new "electronic frontier."
- An interim system, intended to serve some parts of the education and research community until a fully capable NII is offered by the communication and information industry.

The existing Internet has exhibited all of those characteristics at some time or other. But, these characterizations distract the debate from a bigger and more important issue. We need to focus on the question of how to maximize public benefits from the new information infrastructure, whatever form it may finally take. To provide such benefits, we need to develop a clear, consistent and conceptual vision of what an NREN is and is not, and how it would be organized, funded and managed.

The Multi-Faceted Structure of NII

The infrastructure, as it has evolved conceptually over the last few years in the political debate, can be thought of as composed of three different network systems, interconnected and serving somewhat overlapping constituencies. Figure 1 [not available] illustrates the network as a set of three layers. The vertical dimension roughly represents technological sophistication, and the horizontal metric represents the size of the intended base of users, although, as the figure suggests, some overlap exists.

The "High Technology" Research Segment

The top layer is a collection of specialized, ultra-high-speed data communication systems, the most advanced state of the art communications technology. These systems are the true multi-gigabit networks. They are in large part experimental and serve academic and industrial researchers by providing leading-edge services-interconnecting supercomputer centers; carrying data from large, data-intensive research instruments; or connecting researchers in geographically distributed projects.

Technologically, these networks are, for the most part, custom designed and built. They push the state of the art far beyond what is commercially available; and, in many cases, they serve as test-beds for possible future commercial service offerings.

The "Pure NREN"

This segment of the infrastructure provides a wide range of digital data communication services not only to scientific researchers and educators, but also to students and scholars in all fields. Users would access the network principally through its client institutions—colleges and schools at all levels, libraries, museums, and industrial research laboratories.

Networks would offer access to a variety of educational and public information services and resources, formal and informal education, virtual museums, public health services, and access to a variety of government social services and databases.

These networks would provide specialized public information services over high-speed commercially contracted communication lines. Although the pure NREN would be accessible from the switched telephone network, services that depended on the higher data rates and specialized services offered by the network would not necessarily be available, or they would be accessible only in limited form through that interface.

The Universal Infrastructure

The universal infrastructure will extend digital data communications to every home and office—even, if technological trends continue, to every coat pocket. The technological parameters of this network, or set of networks, are difficult to predict at this time; however, the network would no doubt replace the existing telephone system. Depending on its capacity and speed (as well as regulatory decisions), it could also incorporate a large proportion of the existing cable and broadcast infrastructure. Thus, the political battle over who will build the network and who will provide services over it has become extraordinarily intense.

The universal network would reflect a compromise between the desire to make a national infrastructure as sophisticated and long-lasting as possible, and the need to make it broadly affordable and accessible to all people. The need for such a compromise will likely result in a national network of universal, but limited capabilities, coupled with an assortment of more sophisticated services to which access will be limited by price, by geographic location, or by other characteristics.

The Nature of the NREN: A Public Interest Network

The second layer, the NREN (or whatever it may be called), might be thought of as the public interest segment of the future information infrastructure. It will serve certain universal service needs that are not met by simple physical access to the network fiber.

In the traditional phone system, universal service has been relatively easy to provide for. Two characteristics of the system, low cost and physical access to the network, were key. Attachment to the network at a reasonable price meant access to the service-switched voice telephony to everyone else on the network. The service and the network were, in essence, the same.

In the case of the NII, the picture will not be nearly as simple. To assure low cost, physical connection to the network should remain an achievable technical and economic goal. But, access to the physical infrastructure will in no way imply access to all of the resources and services of the network. Voice telephony will certainly be one of the offerings, but improved voice is not why so many are promoting the NII. They expect the network to support a large smorgasbord of new information services, from high definition television to digital libraries.

These services will be layered on top of a complex physical communication infrastructure. In a sense, the physical data communication infrastructure can be thought of as a huge box of tinker toys that users and service providers will assemble together in a wide variety of information services. These services may be offered by the carriers, by the information industry (book publishers, newspapers and the like), by non-profit organizations, and by local, state and federal governments. Some services may be cooperatively purchased and operated by groups of users.

Many of these services, layered on top of the physical communication system, will, themselves, look like higher-level information networks. Examples abound on the current telephone facility. Modern automated teller machine networks, private corporate networks, and commercial services such as Prodigy and CompuServe are now in every sense of the word, "networks," even though they do not string their own wires around the country. Just as in the case of these current examples, many, if not most of these higher-level networks will be private—closed to general public access or available only at a price.

Universal service, to the extent it makes any sense at all in the NII context, must imply inexpensive and easy access by the public to at least some basic set of information resources and services, whether they are provided by the private marketplace, by government, or by non-profit entities of various kinds.

A century ago, the federal government encouraged development of the American West through several legislative acts, including the Homestead Act and the Agricultural Extension Act. (Our era is surely not the first time the government has seen fit to intervene directly in the private marketplace in the name of economic development.) In the Homestead Act it designated Federal land to private ownership and development.

However, that law also required that certain tracts of land be dedicated to public use. Similarly, in the Agricultural Extension Act, the Federal government created institutions, the land-grant colleges, to conduct research and to provide for a free flow of useful information to the agricultural community. Thus, systems of public institutions were created to accompany a private sector oriented infrastructure development.

The two-hundred-year history of infrastructure building in this country is replete with such pragmatic bargains. We turn to the commercial marketplace as the engine of investment and economic growth, but a concomitant recognition of public interest is extracted in return. Intellectual property law is an example. The system of copyright and patent protections called for in the U.S. Constitution were designed as such a bargain. A set of limited information property rights were established specifically to encourage greater public access to information, arts, and invention.

NREN as a Confederation

If the above argument is correct, then NREN as a monolithic government-funded network, a concept many saw imbedded in the 1991 HPCC Act, may never exist. Rather, NREN will be contained within a loose, but interconnected, confederation of public interest networks. Many of these specialized networks are starting to appear in early stages: so-called "freenets" serving local communities, special interest bulletin boards on the Internet, library networks and educational services, state government networks, and regional and national cooperative non-profit networks serving educational and research users. The information and telecommunication industries will also find markets within this mixture of public service networks, although for the private sector, the most profitable information markets will likely remain in the areas of mass entertainment and business information.

The United States has numerous examples in which publicly funded or partially subsidized activities coexist in a politically uneasy but manageable relationship with the private sector. Public transportation, government publishing, public schools, public libraries, parcel post, and public broadcasting are all models of direct government activities. In many other cases, non-profit private institutions—theaters, schools, libraries, research organizations, and the like—that provide public services receive subsidies in the form of tax exemption.

Similarly, there is a need for one or more national institutions to coordinate and support the development of public interest networks. Such institutions could play several roles

- Contracting and managing the collective purchase of commercial services for its user community
- Encouraging and assisting the development of local community computing networks
- Developing new public service applications in areas such as education, health, and public information
- Establishing higher-level interconnection and interface protocols and standards
- Assisting users through education, training, and consulting programs
- Serving as a national voice for public interest networking in the ongoing communications policy debate.

Government funding is certainly appropriate, even necessary, to support certain functions such as applications development and user education; however, these institutions would also need to have significant private support. They need to be insulated from undue political interference. More importantly, serious First Amendment issues could arise were the federal government too substantively close to the operation and management of public information networks. With some few exceptions, it is generally none of the government's business what citizens say to each other or do on such networks.

What Should Be the Governmental Role?

The "why" of government interest in promoting public interest networking is clear. Many public sector, government supported services such as education, public information, R&D, public health, and distribution of financial benefits such as social security, Medicare, or welfare are, basically, information activities. They will benefit greatly from, if not absolutely require, access to the wide array of state of the art communication and information technology that will be part of a new NII. Use of new technology could not only improve service but provide efficiencies and operational savings. Thus, governments at all levels need to see that the NII grows in such a way as to be accessible for these purposes.

More broadly, the potential contribution of a new fundamental communications medium to our social and economic well-being is such that the nation needs to assure that two diverse public interests are protected:

1. The need for broad public access to the dominant knowledge and communication streams in our society,
2. The right of individuals to enjoy privacy in their communications and to freely contract among themselves for the sale or exchange of information goods and services.

These goals may seem to conflict. Public distribution of information competes with the private marketplace, for example. However, there is no reason why both interests cannot be accommodated on the NII. In a town, for example, private lands adjoin public parks. A walk around a city of any size brings one past a library, a bookstore, and a religious reading room handing out free information, and a government publication outlet. All, in a sense, compete with one another. On the other hand, all are necessary for a free, literate, democratic society.

History of technology shows us that a complex relationship can exist between public policy and invention, with no simple distinctions between public and private responsibility in exploiting technology and publicizing its use.

For example, in his book, *The Discoverers* (Random House, 1983), Daniel Boorstin contrasts the evolution of the clock and its enormous impact on Western culture with its minimal impact in the East. So fundamental was this invention to European thought that Boorstin refers to it as the "Mother of machines" (a term coined, we should note, before the Gulf War).

In Europe, the clock underlay the basic transformation of medieval society, the Renaissance, the birth of science, and eventually, the start of industrial revolution. It became the basic metaphor of the universe to astronomers. It brought order to medieval life. Every town had its church steeple or town hall with the large clock telling everyone the hours.

> No self-respecting European town would be without its public clock, which tolled all citizens together to defend, to celebrate, to mourn. A community that could focus its resources in a dazzling public clock was that much more of a community. The bell tolled for all and each, as the poet John Donne noted in 1623, and the tolling of the community's bells was a reminder that "I am involved in humanity." [p. 73]

In the Orient, clocks remained the expensive private toys of the aristocracy and, thus, had little effect on society. In fact, some aspects of clocks were held as state secrets, the sole preserve of the emperor.

The adoption of the clock as a "public technology" in the West went hand in hand with their widespread public use, which, in turn stimulated development of an industry and broad marketplace for timepieces.

In due course, each citizen wanted his own private clocks—first, for his household, then for his person. When more people had their private timepieces, more other people needed timepieces to fulfill their neighbors' expectations at worship, at work, and at play. [p. 73]

The Bargain

The political bargain necessary to preserve public interest in a new NII seems straightforward.

1. Public interest networks (PINs) will need the digital infrastructure that can be built and managed only by private communications companies.
2. The communications companies need some assurance of return before they make the massive investments necessary to build the NII. To get that assurance, they want some degree of market stability and they want to get into the higher-level information service business, where many experts think the real profits will be.

There would seem to be the seeds of a political bargain here, but some mutual suspicion makes it difficult. Stakeholder perceptions of their future roles differ. The PINs see themselves as consumers of telecommunication services and, in many cases, as the leading edge developers of new services and applications. The users they serve—schools, libraries, local government agencies, etc.—doubt that they will any time soon (if ever) be viewed as an attractive and lucrative market by private sector providers.

The companies, however, wishing to enter the information market, see these rapidly growing PINs as potential competitors, growing with the aid of government subsidy and distorting the marketplace for future services. They point to the exponential growth in Internet use, some of it corporate use, and ask where the boundaries are between public and private investments.

The Federal government is inevitably being drawn into the role of referee in this fight. The political stakes are high for a misstep on either side. Clearly, especially in the current political climate, government would be loath to threaten private sector investment in the new infrastructure. On the other hand, government ought to be equally loath to see a new NII develop without the appropriate universal information services that serve the broad public sector responsibilities of government and serve to equalize economic and social opportunity in our society.

The current problem from the public interest perspective is that the threat to private sector investment is concrete, precise, and understandable. The second danger, inadequate attention to the public interest, is still hard to explain and justify, especially in an era where the driving political cliché is, "It's the economy, stupid!"

At the same time, the danger is no less real. The future quality of life in our society—economic, social and individual—will depend in part on the ability of all to participate in the dominant information flows of our society. We have always striven to keep barriers to access low.

Many know the familiar Emily Dickinson line, "There is no frigate like a book." Fewer can cite the last lines of that poem:

> *This traverse may the poorest take*
> *Without oppress of toll;*
> *How frugal is the chariot*
> *That bears the human soul.*

Appendix C:
Access to Electronic Information, Services, and Networks

An Interpretation of the Library Bill of Rights (Draft)

American Library Association

Freedom of expression is an inalienable human right and the foundation for self-government. Freedom of expression encompasses the freedom of speech and the corollary right to receive information. These rights extend to children as well as adults.

Libraries and librarians exist to facilitate these rights by providing access to, identifying, retrieving, organizing, and preserving recorded expression regardless of the formats or technologies in which that expression is recorded.

It is the nature of information that it flows freely across boundaries and barriers despite attempts by individuals, governments, and private entities to channel or control its flow. Electronic technology has increased the speed and universality of this flow.

Although we live in a global information village, many persons do not have access to electronic information sources because of economic circumstances, capabilities of technology, and infrastructure disparity. The degree of access to electronic information divides people into groups of haves and have-nots. Librarians, entrusted as a profession with the stewardship of the public good of free expression, are uniquely positioned to address the issues raised by technological change.

Librarians address intellectual freedom from a strong ethical base and an abiding commitment to the preservation of the individual's rights.

The American Library Association has expressed these basic principles of librarianship in its Code of Ethics and in the Library Bill of Rights and its Interpretations. These serve to guide professional librarians and library governing bodies in addressing issues of intellectual freedom and the rights of the people they serve.

The constant emergence and change of issues arising from the still-developing technology of computer-mediated information generation, distribution, and retrieval need to be approached by librarians from a context of established policy and constitutional principles so that fundamental and traditional tenets of librarianship are not swept away.

In making decisions on how to offer access to electronic information, each library should consider its mission, goals, objectives, cooperative agreements, and the needs of all the people it serves. The library should address the rights of users, the equity of access, and information resources and access issues.

The Rights of Users

All library system and network policies, procedures or regulations relating to electronic resources and services should be scrutinized for potential violation of user rights.

User policies should be developed according to the policies and guidelines established by the American Library Association, including *Guidelines for the Development and Implementation of Policies, Regulations and Procedures Affecting Access to Library Materials, Services and Facilities.*

Users have the right to be free of interference and unreasonable limitations or conditions set by libraries, librarians, system administrators, vendors, network service providers, or others. This specifically includes contracts, agreements, and licenses entered into by libraries on behalf of their users.

No user should be restricted or denied access for expressing or receiving constitutionally protected speech. No user's access should be changed without due process, including, but not limited to, notice and a means of appeal.

Users have a right to full descriptions of and access to the documentation about all electronic systems and programs they are using, and the training and assistance necessary to operate the hardware and software.

Users have the right of confidentiality in all of their activities with electronic resources and services provided by the library, and the library shall ensure that this confidentiality is maintained. The library should support, by policy, procedure, and practice, the user's right to privacy. Users should be advised, however, that security is technically difficult to achieve and that electronic communications and files are safest when they are treated as if they were public.

The rights of users who are minors shall in no way be abridged.

Equity of Access

Electronic information, services, and networks provided directly or indirectly by the library should be readily, equally, and equitably accessible to all library users. Once the decision is made to use library funds to provide access to electronic information, the user must not be required to pay to obtain the information or use the service. When resources are insufficient to meet demand, rationing service may be necessary to provide equitable access. All library policies should be scrutinized in light of *Economic Barriers to Information Access: An Interpretation of the Library Bill of Rights*.

Information Resources and Access Issues

Electronic resources provide unprecedented opportunities to expand the scope of information available to users. Libraries and librarians should provide material and information presenting all points of view. This pertains to electronic resources, no less than it does to the more traditional sources of information in libraries.[1]

Libraries and librarians should not deny or limit access to information available via electronic resources because of its allegedly controversial content or because of the librarian's personal beliefs or fear of confrontation. Information retrieved or utilized electronically should be considered constitutionally protected unless determined otherwise by a court with appropriate jurisdiction.

Providing access to electronic information, services, and networks is not the same thing as selecting and purchasing material for a library collection. Libraries may discover that some material accessed electronically may not meet a library's selection or collection development policy. It is, therefore, left to each user to determine what is appropriate. Parents who are concerned about their children's use of electronic resources should provide guidance to their own children.[2]

Just as libraries do not endorse the viewpoints or vouch for the accuracy or authenticity of traditional materials in the collection, they do not do so for electronic information.

Libraries must support access to all materials on all subjects that serve the needs or interests of all users regardless of the user's age or the content of material. Libraries and librarians should not limit access to information on the grounds that it is perceived to be frivolous or lacking value.

Libraries have a particular obligation to provide access to government publications available only in electronic format.

[1]See *Diversity in Collection Development: An Interpretation of the Library Bill of Rights*.
[2]See *Free Access to Libraries for Minors: An Interpretation of the Library Bill of Rights; Access to Resources and Services in the School Library Media Program;* and *Access for Children and Young People to Videotapes and Other Nonprint Formats*.

Libraries may need to expand their selection or collection development policies to reflect the need to preserve materials central to the library's mission as a retrievable copy in an appropriate format to prevent loss of the information.

Conclusion

By applying traditional tenets of intellectual freedom to new media, librarians provide vision and leadership in an arena where it is so clearly needed. Our services have never been more important.

James Madison wrote, "A popular government, without popular information, or the means of acquiring it, is but a Prologue to a Farce or a Tragedy; or perhaps both. Knowledge will forever govern ignorance; and a people who mean to be their own Governors must arm themselves with the power which knowledge gives."

Appendix D: A Bill of Rights and Responsibilities for Electronic Learners

American Association for Higher Education

PREAMBLE

In order to protect the rights and recognize the responsibilities of individuals and institutions, we, the members of the educational community, propose this Bill of Rights and Responsibilities for the Electronic Community of Learners. These principles are based on a recognition that the electronic community is a complex subsystem of the educational community founded on the values espoused by that community. As new technology modifies the system and further empowers individuals, new values and responsibilities will change this culture. As technology assumes an integral role in education and lifelong learning, technological empowerment of individuals and organizations becomes a requirement and right for students, faculty, staff, and institutions, bringing with it new levels of responsibility that individuals and institutions have to themselves and to other members of the educational community.

ARTICLE I: INDIVIDUAL RIGHTS

The original Bill of Rights explicitly recognized that all individuals have certain fundamental rights as members of the national community. In the same way, the citizens of the electronic community of learners have fundamental rights that empower them.

Section 1. A citizen's access to computing and information resources shall not be denied or removed without just cause.

Section 2. The right to access includes the right to appropriate training and tools required to effect access.

The Bill of Rights and Responsibilities for Electronic Learners is reproduced with permission of the American Association for Higher Education (AAHE). For further information about the Bill or the AAHE Rights & Responsibilities Project contact Frank W. Connolly, 125 Clark Hall, The American University, Washington, D.C. 20016. Phone: (202) 885-3164, Internet: Frank@American.edu.

Section 3. All citizens shall have the right to be informed about personal information that is being and has been collected about them, and have the right to review and correct that information. Personal information about a citizen shall not be used for other than the express purpose of its collection without the explicit permission of that citizen.

Section 4. The constitutional concept of freedom of speech applies to citizens of electronic communities.

Section 5. All citizens of the electronic community of learners have ownership rights over their own intellectual works.

ARTICLE II: INDIVIDUAL RESPONSIBILITIES

Just as certain rights are given to each citizen of the electronic community of learners, each citizen is held accountable for his or her actions. The interplay of rights and responsibilities within each individual and within the community engenders the trust and intellectual freedom that form the heart of our society. This trust and freedom are grounded on each person's developing the skills necessary to be an active and contributing citizen of the electronic community. These skills include an awareness and knowledge about information technology and the uses of information and an understanding of the roles in the electronic community of learners.

Section 1. It shall be each citizen's personal responsibility to actively pursue needed resources: to recognize when information is needed, and to be able to find, evaluate, and effectively use information.

Section 2. It shall be each citizen's personal responsibility to recognize (attribute) and honor the intellectual property of others.

Section 3. Since the electronic community of learners is based upon the integrity and authenticity of information, it shall be each citizen's personal responsibility to be aware of the potential for and possible effects of manipulating electronic information: to understand the fungible nature of electronic information; and to verify the integrity and authenticity, and assure the security of information that he or she compiles or uses.

Section 4. Each citizen, as a member of the electronic community of learners, is responsible to all other citizens in that community: to respect and value the rights of privacy for all; to recognize and respect the diversity of the population and opinion in the community; to behave ethically; and to comply with legal restrictions regarding the use of information resources.

Section 5. Each citizen, as a member of the electronic community of learners, is responsible to the community as a whole to understand what information technology resources are available, to recognize that the members of the community share them, and to refrain from acts that waste resources or prevent others from using them.

ARTICLE III: RIGHTS OF EDUCATIONAL INSTITUTIONS

Educational institutions have legal standing similar to that of individuals. Our society depends upon educational institutions to educate our citizens and advance the development of knowledge. However, in order to survive, educational institutions must attract financial and human resources. Therefore, society must grant these institutions the rights to the electronic resources and information necessary to accomplish their goals.

Section 1. The access of an educational institution to computing and information resources shall not be denied or removed without just cause.

Section 2. Educational institutions in the electronic community of learners have ownership rights over the intellectual works they create.

Section 3. Each educational institution has the authority to allocate resources in accordance with its unique institutional mission.

ARTICLE IV: INSTITUTIONAL RESPONSIBILITIES

Just as certain rights are assured to educational institutions in the electronic community of learners, so too each is held accountable for the appropriate exercise of those rights to foster the values of society and to carry out each institution's mission. This interplay of rights and responsibilities within the community fosters the creation and maintenance of an environment wherein trust and intellectual freedom are the foundation for individual and institutional growth and success.

Section 1. The institutional members of the electronic community of learners have a responsibility to provide all members of their community with legally acquired computer resources (hardware, software, networks, data bases, etc.) in all instances where access to or use of the resources is an integral part of active participation in the electronic community of learners.

Section 2. Institutions have a responsibility to develop, implement, and maintain security procedures to insure the integrity of individual and institutional files.

Section 3. The institution shall treat electronically stored information as confidential. The institution shall treat all personal files as confidential, examining or disclosing the contents only when authorized by the owner of the information, approved by the appropriate institutional official, or required by local, state or federal law.

Section 4. Institutions in the electronic community of learners shall train and support faculty, staff, and students to effectively use information technology. Training includes skills to use the resources, to be aware of the existence of data repositories and techniques for using them, and to understand the ethical and legal uses of the resources.

August 1993

About the Contributors

Mike Godwin is online counsel for the Electronic Frontier Foundation, where he advises users of electronic networks about their legal rights and responsibilities, instructs criminal lawyers and law-enforcement personnel about computer civil-liberties issues, and conducts seminars about civil liberties in electronic communication. Godwin has published articles for print and electronic publications on topics such as electronic searches and seizures, the First Amendment and electronic publications, and the application of international law to computer communications. He has contributed to *The Whole Earth Review, The Quill, Index on Censorship, Internet World, Wired, Playboy,* and *Time,* and is an adjunct professor at the School of Visual Arts in New York. Godwin is a graduate of the University of Texas School of Law where he served as editor-in-chief of *The Daily Texan.*

Laura Lape is associate professor at Syracuse University's College of Law, where she teaches property, intellectual property, and copyright. Before joining the faculty at Syracuse, she practiced law in Boston and taught at the law schools of the University of North Carolina at Chapel Hill and at Temple in Philadelphia. Her undergraduate degree is in Greek from Smith, and she earned an M.A. in Classics at the University of North Carolina at Chapel Hill in 1985. She also received a J.D. from UNC in 1986, summa cum laude, and served on the law review there. Recent papers have been published in *Albany Law Review, Villanova Law Review* and *Dickinson Law Review.* The article in the latter was selected for republication in the 1995 *Intellectual Property Law Review.*

Marlyn Kemper Littman is professor at the School of Computer and Information Sciences, Nova Southeastern University, in Fort Lauderdale, Florida. Her interest in network security originated with her text *Networking: Choosing a LAN Path to Interconnection* (Scarecrow, 1987). She teaches doctoral courses in computer networks, telecommunications, emerging technologies and multimedia. Her courses are delivered in the distance education mode, via computer. In May 1995 she gave a presentation on "The Perils of Network Security" at the 16th National Online Meeting in New York City. Author of many articles on technology and its applications, Littman is currently focusing her research on the issues, ethics, and problems of security in online systems.

Jorge Reina Schement is associate professor at Rutgers SCILS, as well as in the Department of Puerto Rican and Hispanic Caribbean Studies. At the invitation of the chairman of the Federal Communications Commission, he served as director of the F.C.C.'s Information Policy Project in 1994. His latest publications include *Tendencies and Tensions of the Information Age: The Production and Distribution of Information in the United States* (Transaction, 1995), and *Toward an Information Bill of Rights and Responsibilities* (The Aspen Institute, forthcoming).

Jana Varlejs is associate professor at Rutgers SCILS, and has been involved in planning the annual symposia and editing the proceedings since 1982. Director of SCILS' Professional Development Studies from 1979 to 1993, her research interests lie primarily in the area of librarians' continuing learning.